AF571905

This Basic Bible Series study was developed through the combined efforts and resources of a number of David C. Cook's dedicated lesson writers. It was compiled and edited by Yvonne Schultz, designed by Melanie Lawson and Dawn Lauck, with cover art by Richard Sparks.
—Gary Wilde, Series Editor

ISBN: 1-55513-855-1
Library of Congress Catalog Number: 87-70318

Isaiah 42:6, 7

A light for the Gentiles . . .
to release from the dungeon
those who sit in darkness.

Contents

Introducing Isaiah

With this study of the Book of Isaiah, we approach "the theological high water mark of the whole Old Testament. . . . Not one of the other prophets approaches Isaiah in intellectual vigour or, more particularly, in the magnificent sweep of his ideas" (G. von Rad, *Old Testament Theology, II*). "In his peculiar style, he occupies the same place among the prophets as Solomon among the kings. Under all circumstances, and in whatever state of mind, he is completely master of his materials—simple yet majestic in style—elevated, yet without affectation—and beautiful, though unadorned" (Franz Delitzsch, *Isaiah*). In short, the Book of Isaiah is "recognized as the literary masterpiece of all Hebrew writing" (J. W. Watts, *Old Testament Teaching*).

Isaiah is referred to by New Testament writers more than any other Old Testament book: 590 references from 63 chapters are found in 23 New Testament books.

Irving Jensen has said that, like the whole Bible with its 66 books, Isaiah has 66 chapters. These divide into two basic sections, like the Old and New Testament divisions. Isaiah 1—39 are ominous, whereas chapters 40—66 clearly trumpet the comforting note of grace (*Survey of the Old Testament*). Here is the outline we will follow in this study:

I. Themes of Fruitfulness and Commitment from Isaiah 1—39 (Lessons 1—5)
II. Themes of Comfort from Isaiah 40—66 (Lessons 6—9)
III. Themes of Hope from the Messianic Prophecies (Lessons 10—12)

1

God's Case Against His People

Truth to Apply: As I become more willing to change and to obey Christ, I, along with other Christians, can counteract sinful national influences.

Key Verse: "Come now, let us reason together," says the Lord. "Though your sins are like scarlet, they shall be as white as snow . . ." (Isa. 1:18).

Bob was a "terror" in his small Christian college. The college had many rules, and Bob deliberately tried to break most of them. Some of Bob's pranks were harmless and funny, but most of them were troublesome and nasty. Bob hated to study. He never read a book, and he bragged about his new methods of cheating on exams.

At last Bob was forced to leave school. When he tried to reapply, he was told to attend college elsewhere. If he got good grades at another school and cleaned up his life, then he would be allowed to return.

Then a miracle happened. Bob turned his life over to God. He stopped hurting people and living only for himself. He began seeking ways to serve God through helping others. He started using his brilliant mind at another college.

When Bob returned to the Christian college the following year, he was a totally different person. He became a leader of the student body in academics, in Bible studies, and in service projects.

What had to happen to Bob before he could begin a new approach to life? In your opinion, how much good does a knowledge of moral principles do without a willingness to change?

Background/Overview: *Isaiah 1:2-8, 18-20*

Isaiah's world was full of political and social unrest. Assyria was threatening to swallow Syria, Israel, Judah—even Egypt. The extremely rich lived next door to the extremely poor. The poor were oppressed by land grabbers, unjust rulers, and profiteering schemers. The wealthy class was indulgent in its luxury and idleness, and remained indifferent to the suffering of others.

Isaiah observed a widening divorce between religion and life. Religious devotion had disintegrated into a set of formal practices. The worship of God was thoroughly polluted with the worship of others gods, particularly in the Kingdom of Israel. Soothsayers and diviners were popular. Through all of national life ran a pride and self-complacency that led the people to be casual about their dependence on God.

In Isaiah 1, the prophet carries God's words of judgment and hope to His people. He sees a great chasm between the might and glory of God and the sinfulness of the people. But into the waywardness and sickness of the people, the hope of salvation is injected—if the people are willing to obey.

Light on the Text

The Anger of a Rejected Father (1:2-4)

The first chapter of Isaiah introduces the entire book. It contains the basic themes of Isaiah's ministry: the sinfulness of Judah and Jerusalem (vss. 2-6), the loving and tender appeals of the Lord (vss. 16-19), the certainty of coming judgment (vss. 20, 24, 28-31) and wonderful news of the salvation to come (vss. 26, 27).

1:2 Isaiah is acting as God's plaintiff in this case against His people. Isaiah cries, "Hear, O heavens! Listen, O earth! For the Lord has spoken." As Heaven and earth testified against Israel when God plead with his people to renew their covenant with Him (Deut. 30:19), so Isaiah calls the heavens and the earth to witness his cry for a renewal of right living. As Moses was a prophet, Isaiah is a prophet, but in both cases it is God who speaks.

When God chose Israel, she was a small and insignificant people. From simple beginnings He raised her to a position of eminence. God enlarged the nation and gave her the special gifts of the Law and the prophets. Now, God is angry with Israel because "I reared children and brought them up, but they have rebelled against me."

Against God's free grace and persistent love, the rebellion of the people of Israel stands out in shocking contrast. The imagery here is of a family—children casting aside a loving father.

1:3 The simplest of animals knows to whom it owes allegiance. "The ox knows his master, the donkey his owner's manger," but Israel is acting so foolishly, she cannot even remember her master and preserver. Endowed with spiritual gifts and bestowed with the benefits of God's special revelation, Israel is bested by the animals, which are endowed with neither human intelligence nor God's guidance.

1:4 God then calls His people a "sinful nation, a people loaded with guilt . . . ." Not only do they sin, but they sin constantly and habitually. Israel is loaded with guilt, bowed and weighted down under a burden she is too small to carry. Still, she insists on adding to the weight.

Not only is Israel pictured as burdened by evil, she is seen as causing evil. What should have been a family of righteous individuals has become a brood of evildoers, producing, in their union with one another, more evildoers. The nation was intended to be a holy people. Instead, they have forsaken the Lord. Israel denied her heritage; further, she mocked the Father who had raised her, demonstrating the utmost contempt for the One who loved her so tenderly. There is great pain in this denial, a picture of rebellion that goes beyond a child simply finding her own way in the world to a complete revulsion with all that she has been raised to believe.

Israel has gone so far as to turn her back on the God of Israel!

A Body Covered with Open Sores (1:5-8)

1:5, 6 "Why should you be beaten anymore?" There is no place left to spank! She is covered with wounds, bruises, and sores "from the sole of your foot to the top of your head." Why should Israel, through her sin and unfaithfulness, keep asking for punishment? "Why do you persist in rebellion?" is an interesting commentary on the children of Israel. God is angry with them because of their constant rebellion. Theirs was a condition of revolt, a people who were turned against God. Yet even under the pressure of God's punishment, the people of Israel did not become humble or repentant. They continued to rebel.

1:7, 8 This image of physical suffering is paralleled by the desolation of Israel's land. "Your country is desolate," says Isaiah, "your cities burned with fire; your fields are being stripped by foreigners right before you, laid waste as when overthrown by strangers." Israel is so defeated and desolate that strangers can come in and do anything they want to her cities and fields.

Finally, the desolation is so complete that Isaiah compares the beauty of Jerusalem to a watchman's hut in a field of melons. To this day, one can see these flimsy huts in the melon and cucumber fields of Palestine. Except for a short time at harvest, they stand deserted and useless under the burning sun. The "Daughter of Zion is . . . like a city under siege"—standing, but practically useless, for she is enslaved by her own walls.

Hope from the Lord (1:18-20)

1:18 " 'Come now, let us reason together,' says the Lord." Israel is invited to discuss with God the accusations made against her. He intends to show that "Israel is precisely that sinful nation which God has accused her of being, and also that he is a God willing to forgive," as Edward J. Young (*The Book of Isaiah, I,* Eerdmans, 1972), notes. Sin and rebellion will be shown to be unreasonable.

"Though your sins are like scarlet," the color of blood shed violently, "they shall be as white as snow"—quite the opposite. The poetic parallel, "though they are red as crimson, they shall be like wool," emphasizes the transformation that is possible.

But the promised change carries conditions: willingness and obedience. Without repentance, that change of life which involves a willingness to turn from wickedness to obedience, the promise is ineffective. Is Israel able to *create* willingness and obedience? Hardly; she is covered with sores from the soles of her feet to the top of her head. The ability to fulfill these requirements is the gift of God, His grace. "At the same time, the responsibility of the nation to obey is not lessened. It is the mystery of the free offer of the gospel which here confronts us," says Young.

1:19, 20 If the people are willing and obedient, they "will eat the best from the land," enjoying the benefits of peace and domesticity. But if they insist on rebellion, on persisting in their wicked ways, they "will be devoured by the sword." A nation in a precarious political position, already dismembered by war, could not afford to resist the command of God.

Change from the Inside

There are people who believe that in order to change the way humans are, you need to change the world around them. Of course, change may be slow, they admit, but eventually, if conditions are modified for a long enough period of time, we will have a "new human."

While we as Christians don't discount the influence of environment, we maintain that the only way people truly change is from the inside out. All other change is window dressing that doesn't affect the basic human nature. That can only be changed by God.

How, then, can we best counteract sinful influences in society? By introducing more of our fellow humans to God, and by allowing God to live His life through us.

For Discussion

1. How was the sin of individuals affecting national life (see 1:7-9)? How does the sin of an individual in a place of prominence affect national life today? Think of and discuss an example. What can happen when such an individual repents?

2. In what sense is God's forgiveness unconditional? In what sense does it have conditions? How has this worked in your life? Share and discuss.

3. Where was Israel to find the ability to repent? How has God helped you *want* to obey Him and then given you the ability to follow through?

Window on the Word

Prayer to Follow Through

"Grant, Almighty God, that as Thou hast made known to us Thy law, and hast also added the Gospel, in which Thou callest us to Thy service, and also invitest us with all kindness to partake of Thy grace,—O grant, that we may not be deaf, either to Thy command or to the promises of Thy mercy, but render ourselves submissive to Thee everywhere, and so learn to devote all our faculties to Thee, that we may in truth avow that the rule of a holy and religious life has been delivered to us in Thy Law, and that we may firmly adhere to Thy promises, lest through any of the allurements of the world, or through the flatteries and delusions of Satan, Thou shouldst suffer our minds to be drawn away from that love which Thou hast once for all manifested to us in Thine only-begotten Son, and in which Thou daily confirmest us by the teaching of the Gospel, until we at length shall come to the full enjoyment of this love in that celestial inheritance, which has been purchased for us by the blood of Thine only Son. Amen" (*Devotions and Prayers of John Calvin*, Baker, 1977).

2

The Song of the Vineyard

Truth to Apply: Unproductiveness and unrighteousness will not go unjudged.

Key Verse: The vineyard of the Lord Almighty is the house of Israel, and the men of Judah are the garden of his delight. And he looked for justice, but saw bloodshed; for righteousness, but heard cries of distress (Isa. 5:7).

"A cross, selfish Dog went to rest one hot afternoon in a manger. When the tired Ox came in from the field and wanted to eat his hay, the Dog barked at him so that he dared not try it. 'To keep others from having what they need,' said the Ox to himself, 'when you can't use it yourself, is the meanest selfishness I know' " ("The Dog in the Manger," from Aesop's Fables).

Selfish ambition is entwined among the sins which Isaiah catalogs. When people reject God, they are turning from God to serve themselves. When an individual rejects something God tells her, she is turning from God to do what she wants. How do you most often express selfishness? How do you feel when you realize you have acted selfishly?

Background/Overview: *Isaiah 5:1-23*

We are not certain when Isaiah wrote his "song of the vineyard," but from the details in Isaiah 5:1-7, we may gather that it was written early in Isaiah's career, with war just around the corner. Isaiah addressed his song of God's judgment to Israel, a people living in moral and spiritual decay. Real estate barons greedily gobbled land, drunkards and brawlers were heroes, the arrogant and deceitful flourished. Israel's national security was at stake from without; within, she was deteriorating.

For the Hebrews, vineyards were symbols of prosperity, peace, and security. A newly planted grapevine will not produce for at least two years, and the best grapes come from well-cultivated, new vines that grow from established roots. Isaiah knew the care and attention that a grapevine requires, how the clusters of grapes are sweetest to the person who tended them. So he sings a song, a song of a relationship that should have been sweet, but has turned sour.

Light on the Text

The Prophet Sings a Song (5:1, 2)

Like a folksinger, Isaiah sings to the people. His song is a marvel of rhythmic assonance, where words sound alike but are not true rhymes. So what we read in our English Bibles is a literal translation, not a musical one. The sounds of the Hebrew pairs—*ashirah/shirath, lididi/dodi, kerem/quren*—are unavailable to those of us who have no knowledge of the original language. Regardless, this is a song. If Isaiah were to stand at the corner of Broad and Walnut today, a crowd would gather to hear his fine singing and rich lyrics.

"My loved one had a vineyard," Isaiah sings. His loved one is his good friend, God, though we are not yet told this. Isaiah's good friend selected a plot of fertile ground, with just the right soil mix. In Palestine, this was no small feat. "The Arabs have a proverb to the effect that when God created the world an angel flew over it carrying a bag of stones under each arm," writes Young. "As he flew over Palestine, one bag broke so that half of all the stones in the world are in Palestine."

Isaiah's friend planted the plot with "the choicest vines," excellent stock, healthy and strong, bred for the climate and growing season. Then he built a watchtower, to protect the young vines from intruders. From its protection, the watchmen could oversee the well-being of the vineyard.

Finally, God "cut out a winepress" from the solid stone, an ardous task indeed. Yet even this was done, because God anticipated a rich and bountiful harvest.

Then the love song turns into a tragedy. The owner waits patiently for the harvest, watching the vines grow and the grapes form and become larger. With a good harvest, his labor will have been justified. But the vineyard yields only bad fruit, sour grapes that are just as acidic and flavorless as wild grapes.

What Else Could Have Been Done? (5:3-7)

5:3, 4 The speaker then becomes the owner of the vineyard, who asks for an audience to hear his case. He calls on the "dwellers in Jerusalem," the capital city, where the wickedness of the nation was concentrated. He also calls on the "men of Judah," who lived in other parts of the nation, but who were just as guilty.

Unwittingly, the accused persons, those who yield only bad fruit, have become the jurors of verse 3. Isaiah presents a parable of wrongdoing and then asks who is at fault. By giving the obvious answer, the listeners pass judgemnt on themselves.

"What more could have been done for my vineyard than I have done for it?" asks the owner (vs. 4). The obvious answer: "Nothing; you did everything that could be done." Then, "Why . . . ?" Picture a gaping silence between verses 4 and 5: the listeners are caught. Any answer, spoken with truth, is self-condemnation.

5:5, 6 In an abrupt, impatient shift, the Lord bluntly tells His listeners what He is going to do with His vineyard. The poet builds the strongest impression possible in verses 1-

6 before suddenly and devastatingly revealing the meaning of the symbolism in verse 7. God is going to systematically rip out His vineyard. First to go are the hedge and the wall, the outside protections. With these barriers gone, cattle could enter the vineyard and trample it. In its place will grow briers and thorns, which can survive almost anywhere. The certainty that God is the owner of the vineyard is emphasized, for only God can "command the clouds not to rain on it."

5:7 The song is over; the illustration is finished. The prophet continues where the Lord leaves off. The Lord Almighty has a vineyard. The "house of Israel," which includes both the Northern Kingdom of Israel and the Southern Kingdom of Judah, is "the vineyard of the Lord Almighty." "The men of Judah," specifically the Southern Kingdom, "are the garden of his delight." There were nations other than Israel, but on Israel He set his affection. He took care of her, tenderly cultivating her attributes, and He looked for the good fruit of His work—a harvest of fair business practices, of moderate life-styles, of honesty and integrity, of justice in the courtroom. Instead, He saw materialism (5:8), land exploitation (5:9, 10), brawling and reveling (5:11-14), deceit and wickedness (5:18, 20), arrogance (5:19, 21), bribery and graft (5:23).

A List of Woes (5:8-23)

5:8-10 "Woe to you," says Isaiah. He begins with wealthy landowners who buy up land, squeezing out the poor landowner. Because God had given the people of Israel their land, they were not to become rich at the expense of others. As a result of their sin, the land would become unproductive, yielding less produce than seed sown. It would be useless even to cultivate the soil.

5:11, 12 The abuse of wine was so consuming that the drunkards woke early just to get a good start at it. They drank all the day long and on into the night—with parties and saloon songs. They had the instruments of worship, "harps and lyres . . . tambourines and flutes . . . "—and wine. But "they have no regard for the deeds of the

Lord . . . " (vs. 12). They had lost perspective completely.

5:18, 19 These cynical doubters want God to demonstrate His power without any spiritual change on their part. They were attached to their sin and wickedness, pulling it along behind them like one pulls a puppy. They were fond of their sin; why should they let it go? And why should they let go until they had seen God act?

5:20, 21 "Woe to those who call evil good and good evil." They are so engulfed in darkness that they think it is the light. They become so accustomed to bitterness that they think it is sweetness, and everyone else must have it wrong. "Love God" becomes "Love yourself." "Do not commit adultery" becomes "Every marriage needs an affair." "Do not steal" becomes "Why should I report a little extra income?"

Isaiah pronounces woe on "those who are wise in their own eyes," who are relying on themselves instead of on God to protect and deliver them. "God is a crutch for people who can't stand on their own two feet," they say.

5:22, 23 Isaiah condemns the models that are being emulated. Government officials, instead of ruling justly, were heavy drinkers, ready to "acquit the guilty for a bribe, but deny justice to the innocent" (vs .23). They were more concerned for their own rights than for the rights of others. Yet, they were made national heroes.

For Discussion

1. What is the relationship of the singer to the owner of the vineyard? Who else in the Bible had this relationship with God? Would you describe your relationship with God in this way? Why?

2. Isaiah describes the owner of the vineyard as taking extra, special care of it. How has God taken special care of you? How has He built walls and hedges around you?

3. How did Isaiah confront his listeners with their sin?

How do you suppose they reacted? How have you responded when someone confronted you with a sin?

4. Was there a time when your life-style was only bad fruit? Have you ever produced bad fruit since you turned to God, perhaps a cluster here or a bunch there? What did God do about it? What did you do about it?

5. What aspects of Israel's national life did the bad fruit exemplify? What aspects of the national life of your nation are examples of bad fruit? What can you do to help produce good fruit in your nation's life?

Window on the Word

Where Blindness Is Preferred

There is a story of a man who fell into the lost Country of the Blind. When he realized where he was, he determined to make himself king, believing that the inhabitants would immediately perceive that sight and light were superior to blindness and dark.

" . . . Nunez found himself trying to explain the great world out of which he had fallen, and the sky and mountains and sight and such-like marvels, to these elders who sat in darkness in the Country of the Blind. And they would believe and understand nothing whatever he told them, a thing quite outside his expectation. . . . Blind men of genius had arisen among them and questioned the shreds of belief and tradition they had brought with them from their seeing days, and had dismissed all these things as idle fancies, and replaced them with new and saner explanations. Much of their imagination had shriveled with their eyes, and they had made for themselves new imaginations with their ever more sensitive ears and fingertips. Slowly Nunez realised this; that his expectation of wonder and reverence at his origin and gifts was not to be borne out . . . ."

("The Country of the Blind," *28 Science Fiction Stories of H. G. Wells*, Dover Publications, 1952)

3

A Vision and a Mission

Truth to Apply: I need to understand what God's vision is for me and to apply it in service to Him.

Key Verse: Then I heard the voice of the Lord saying, "Whom shall I send? And who will go for us?" (Isa. 6:8).

In my first year in Hong Kong, I met Ruth, an attractive and pleasant young missionary (to China) from South Dakota. Usually in a conversation or two I can learn what a person's mission and denominational background are. But with Ruth I could not tell. There were no clues. She was engrossed with her present work—and she was effective. My curiosity got the best of me, and one day I asked directly.

"What mission board are you with?"

"None."

Hmmm. "Who sent you?"

"God," with perfect humility—no self-consciousness.

"How did you know what to do? You know—where to live, what language course to take, and all that orientation bit?"

"I graduated from Bible school and knew I wanted to be a missionary to the Chinese. So I came."

"How are you supported?"

"By my church."

"Ah, then they sent you."

"Yes, I suppose you could say that. Yes, God and my church sent me."

The last I heard was that God had sent her a most suitable husband, and together they are happily serving the God who sends. (Ada Lum, *A Hitchhiker's Guide to Missions*, InterVarsity Press, 1984)

Is Ruth typical? Should such certainty of vision and mission be typical? Why or why not?

Background/Overview: *Isaiah 6:1-8*

The earliest meaning of "holiness" in the Old Testament was that of "separateness." In the centuries following the Mosaic period of Jewish history, Israelite awareness focused on three other aspects of holiness. They became aware that holy was closely related with divine. It was seen as a primary characteristic of God that includes all his other attributes.

Second, the Israelites recognized that God shares His holiness. Isaiah confirmed this when he said, "For this is what the high and lofty One says—. . . 'I live in a high and holy place, but also with him who is contrite and lowly in spirit . . . " (Isa. 57:15).

The third development of Israelite understanding about holiness is its absolute opposition to evil. Humanity experiences alienation from God and the loss of His favor as a result of moral failure. Isaiah's conviction of personal and natural sin (Isa. 6:5) was a direct product of his awareness of God's holiness.

Nevertheless, the people of Israel are God's holy people (Ex. 22:31) not because of their righteousness but because of God's. Only as God exchanges His own holiness for human sin are people made acceptable to God. The more we seek to understand the mysteries of grace, the more we should be filled with wonder and love for that pure Love who sought us out.

Light on the Text

Isaiah's Vision of God (6:1-4)

6:1, 2 "In the year that King Uzziah died" tells us when Isaiah had his vision—about 739 B.C. King Uzziah's death came at a crucial point in Judah's history. "The great glory and national pride of Judah were now facing an end, never to rise again. . . . From now on Judah declined more and more, and Rome increased," writes Young.

At this critical time, Isaiah saw the Lord. Three things about God struck Isaiah (vs. 1):

1) He was "seated on a throne," the place of both king and judge. He was ready to pronounce judgment on the people over whom He ruled.

2) He was "high and exalted," demonstrating His high position over the people. Isaiah perhaps saw the Lord sitting on His throne in Heaven, an interpretation which the context favors.

3) "And the train of his robe filled the temple," as God ruled with royalty and majesty.

Hovering above God's throne were seraphs (vs. 2), or "burning ones." Young describes them as "personal, spiritual beings, for they have faces, feet and hands, they employ speech and understand moral concepts." They are always present, always ready to attend to His every request. Their continuous occupation is the work of praising God (vs. 3). They sing praises antiphonally, calling back and forth to one another, like a choir. Perhaps for Isaiah's benefit, they used human language.

6:3, 4 "Holy, holy, holy is the Lord Almighty," they sang (vs. 3). The repetition seems primarily to be for emphasis, as when a child stomps her foot and cries, "No, no, no!" The stress on the holiness of God in this passage is significant. Since Isaiah speaks of "the Holy One" 26 times in his writings, it is obvious that the vision made a deep impression on him. Recalling his encounter with God undoubtedly helped him to endure the hard times which came later in his ministry as he experienced Israel's cold response to the message he brought. God, in all of His holiness, stands in stark contrast to sinning people. Isaiah saw this contrast as he stood dumbfounded and watched the seraphs ministering to the Holy One and proclaiming His greatness.

William Evans came to the heart of the matter when he observed, "Our view of the necessity of the atonement will depend very largely upon our view of the holiness of God" (*The Great Doctrines of the Bible*). It is important that non-Christians catch a glimpse of the vision that Isaiah had. They need to realize that God and any form of evil or impurity are totally incompatible. The Bible makes it clear that God is entirely opposed to anything that is evil. Anything that could defile Him or any of His creatures is repugnant to His very nature. And He calls out to us, saying, "I am the Lord your God; consecrate yourselves and be holy, because I am holy" (Lev. 11:44). Separation from God comes because of human sin, as Isaiah later in his ministry reminded Israel (Isa. 59:1, 2).

"The whole earth is full of his glory" brings to mind the Psalms (e.g., 8:18) where the writer speaks of God's hand in His Creation. "The heavens declare the glory of God; the skies proclaim the work of his hands," wrote David. "Their voice goes out into all the earth, their words to the ends of the world" (Ps. 19:1, 4). His glory is disclosed in the arena of the earth, where the struggles between light and dark take place. The Son of Righteousness rules over the Prince of Darkness. The whole earth, the physical and the spiritual world, are influenced by His glory.

The praise of the seraphs was so great that "at the sound of their voices the doorposts and thresholds shook and the temple was filled with smoke" (vs. 4). God's holiness justifies such praise and adoration from a host of angelic beings. The presence of smoke is regarded as a natural attendant of the fire on the altar. As Isaiah saw it, he would be filled with solemn reverence and awe, for he would have known he was in the presence of God.

Isaiah's Mission for God (6:5-8)

6:5, 6 Confronted by the holiness of God, Isaiah cried out in alarm. He probably feared for his life, for to see the Lord in all of His glory was something to be feared (see Ex. 33:20; Jdg. 13:22). "I am ruined!" he cried. He was undone, destroyed, dissolved. Isaiah suddenly became aware of how frail he was as he stood before God. Regardless of any specific sin he may have been thinking of, he was "a man of unclean lips, [living] among a people of unclean lips" (vs. 5). He, like all humans, was a sinner; he was, as we all are, completely surrounded by sinners. Isaiah felt a deep sense of his sin and of utter helplessness to do anything about it. When he saw "the King, the Lord Almighty," he became acutely conscious of this.

God initiated a rite of purification (vs. 6). One of the seraphs flew to Isaiah "with a live coal in his hand, which he had taken with tongs from the altar." Cleansing was symbolized by the application of the hot coal to Isaiah's mouth. With this act, his guilt was taken away and his sin atoned for. But the deed itself was not the important thing; God alone is the purifier. Without cleansing—repentance, forgiveness, atonement—Isaiah was unfit for God's service, just as we are unfit until we are cleansed.

6:7, 8 For the first time in the vision, the Lord speaks (vs. 8). He begins by asking two rhetorical questions, "Whom shall I send? And who will go for us?" God need consult only with Himself, thus He indicates in His question that He is a plurality of persons. Isaiah's prophecy is the most Christological of all the Old Testament books. He had to form his awareness of the Messiah from God, and perhaps this was the occasion when further understanding of God's nature developed.

God Himself gives the commission, and He expects a response from Isaiah. Whom? Among all the inhabitants of earth, among all the people of Judah, whom shall He send? And who will go?

Isaiah's response is direct and immediate. Now that he has been prepared, he is ready to do service for the Lord. Even before he knows precisely what God wants him to do, he is ready.

Hearing God's Call

In Western culture, we have developed the techniques of analysis that account for our growing mastery of nature and the intricate advances in science and technology. Along with that we have increasingly tended to view the human as a complex machine. This has filtered into our common life in many ways, among them the proliferation of principles, techniques, for succeeding in everything from marriage to prayer. The principles themselves are not necessarily wrong; in many cases they have been enormously helpful. What is troubling is the tendency to treat even spiritual things as if they were extensions of the material, to be controlled and manipulated.

The problem with that is that the life of the spirit has rules of its own that are often incompatible with material goals. One important difference is that the spiritual life calls for a continual emptying of selfishness, a self-giving, whereas success in the material world calls for a gathering of personal power to manipulate and control objects.

When we approach any area of spiritual life, including mission, let us sensitize ourselves to God's leading, being willing to set aside ways that we might do things for better ways that He might show us. By all means, let us respond to God's call, but let us respond in deep awareness of our own sinfulness and of our need for a thorough reorientation in our thinking and life values.

For Discussion

1. What is the scene as the vision begins in verse 1? Why do you think this physical description was important to the vision? What characteristics or attributes of God are emphasized?

2. What is the role of the seraphs? What is the primary purpose of all who serve God? How do you express your praise to God in the jobs that God has given you to do?

3. Why did the seraphs emphasize the holiness of God? How have you remembered God's holiness in your local church life? in your family life? in your devotional life?

4. How have you seen "the whole earth" filled with the glory of God? What do you think would happen if God withdrew from His creation?

5. Do you think Isaiah was speaking of a specific sin he had committed, or was he saying that he was a sinner? What should be the content of our confessions of sin before God? Is Isaiah's cry one that is applicable to us?

6. How did Isaiah respond to God's questions? How might he have responded? Are there ways in which God has asked you the same questions? How did you respond? Do you know anyone who has said, "I'm not available. Don't send me"? What were the consequences of this decision?

Three Leaps for Joy

"Now I saw in my dream, that the highway up which Christian was to go, was fenced on either side with a wall, and that wall was called Salvation. Up this way, therefore, did burdened Christian run, but not without great difficulty, because of the load on his back.

"He ran thus till he came at a place somewhat ascending; and upon that place stood a Cross, and a little below, in the bottom, a sepulchre. So I saw in my dream, that just as Christian came up with the Cross, his burden loosed from off his shoulders, and fell from off his back, and began to tumble, and so continued to do, till it came to the mouth of the sepulchre, where it fell in, and I saw it no more.

"Then was Christian glad and lightsome, and said with a merry heart, He hath given me rest by his sorrow, and life by his death. Then he stood still a while, to look and wonder, for it was very surprising to him that the sight of the cross should thus ease him of his burden. He looked, therefore, and looked again, even till the springs that were in his head sent the waters down his cheeks. Now as he stood looking and weeping, behold, three shining ones came to him, and saluted him with, 'Peace be to thee': so the first said to him, 'Thy sins be forgiven thee'; the second stripped him of his rags, and clothed him with change of raiment; the third also set a mark on his forehead, and gave him a roll with a seal upon it, which he bid him look on as he ran, and that he should give it in at the celestial gate: so they went their way. Then Christian gave three leaps for joy, and went on singing . . .

Blest cross! blest sepulchre! blest rather be
The Man that there was put to shame for me!"

(John Bunyan, *The Pilgrim's Progress*, Reiner Publications, 1974)

4

Turn to the Lord

Truth to Apply: My deepest trust must be in God, not in my own strength.

Key Verse: This is what the Sovereign Lord, the Holy One of Israel, says: "In repentance and rest is your salvation, in quietness and trust is your strength, but you would have none of it" (Isa. 30:15).

"They are not something we do, they are something we are, and therein lies both their subtlety and their power.

To be specific, the self-sins are these: self-righteousness, self-pity, self-confidence, self-sufficiency, self-admiration, self-love and a host of others like them. They dwell too deep within us and are too much a part of our natures to come to our attention till the light of God is focused upon them. The grosser manifestations of these sins, egotism, exhibitionism, self-promotion, are strangely tolerated in Christian leaders even in circles of impeccable orthodoxy. . . . Promoting self under the guise of promoting Christ is currently so common as to excite little notice.

"One should suppose that proper instruction in the doctrines of man's depravity and the necessity for justification through the righteousness of Christ alone would deliver us from the power of self-sins; but it does not work out that way. Self can live unrebuked at the very altar . . . . To tell all the truth, it seems actually to feed upon orthodoxy and is more at home in a Bible conference than in a tavern" (A. W. Tozer, *The Pursuit of God*, Christian Publications).

Do you agree with Tozer? Is he overstating or understating his case? How so? In what areas of your life are you most susceptible to the sin of self-sufficiency?

Background/Overview: *Isaiah 31:1-9*

Franz Delitzsch, coauthor of the Keil and Delitzsch commentaries on the Old Testament, calls chapters 28—33 of Isaiah the "Book of Woes." In five addresses, Isaiah pronounces God's judgment, each beginning with a woe. Israel, Judah, Jerusalem, and Assyria are all judged in these addresses for turning away from God.

These chapters show that the people were seeking independence the wrong way. Instead of depending on God, they were relying on their alliance with Egypt. The Book of Woes traces the development of this faithlessness. God's indictments peak at a fever pitch in chapter 30.

Today's Scripture passage, Isaiah 31, has fewer words and a calmer tone than chapter 30, but the message is the same—judgment against Jerusalem for trusting in Egypt, and God's restoration of His people.

Light on the Text

God's Proclamation (31:1)

God's indictment against Judah can be condensed into a single word—woe. Why was God so upset about a simple treaty with Egypt? In this verse, the shallow reasoning of the Israelites is exposed. They saw many strong horses, chariots and horsemen; they depended on them for help. Because Judah was small, she could not support a cavalry, only an infantry. So the leadership of Judah may have seen the chariots and horsemen as a supplement, a failsafe, for their army. But they had been forbidden to return to Egypt (Deut. 17:16). The Hebrews did not turn to Egypt in a moment of panic, but had developed an habitual reliance on their neighboring country.

But the Holy One is stronger than many horses and chariots, and the invisible God is mightier than Egypt's visible armies. Paul tells us that "what is seen is temporary, but what is unseen is eternal" (II Cor. 4:18). With their history of God's leading, the Israelites should have known this. But in the hour of need, they opted for temporary, finite help.

Though turning to Egypt was, in itself, a problem, what was worse was that they trusted in Egypt without trusting in God. What seemed like a simple treaty was actually a denial of God's ability to protect.

The tone of this woe also contains hurt. Beyond righteous indignation, God feels the kind of hurt any person would feel when a spouse has been unfaithful. He often uses the image of adultery to communicate what He feels about His people's idolatry (see Jdg. 2:17; Ezek. 23:30). In spite of the hurt and rejection, God's love persists. He eventually draws His unfaithful people back to Himself.

God's Power (31:2, 3)

31:2 "Yet he too is wise . . ." is sarcastic and dripping with irony. "You think you're so smart," God seems to be saying. Then He proceeds to put both Israelites and Egyptians in their place in no uncertain terms.

God's wisdom is not demonstrated in an indiscriminate bringing of evil, but in his rising up "against the house of the wicked" (vs. 2). "The house of Jacob (Isa. 2:5), a seed of evildoers (1:4), has now become a house of evildoers. God stands up against such in that he turns against the help that the workers of evil provide," notes Young. "These workers of evil are not the Egyptians, but those in Judah who seek help from man rather than from God." In the next phrase, God pronounces the fall of "those who help evildoers," that is, the Egyptians.

31:3 In quick, slashing statements God exposes the folly and futility of comparing God to anything or anyone else: "But the Egyptians are men and not God; their horses are flesh and not spirit" (vs. 3). God will accomplish His work and punish evildoers. This isn't a whim; it's based on His very nature. Yet the Israelites are treating God as if He were a changeable human being.

Even more arrogant is the Israelites' implied comparison of God's power to Egypt's power. They chose Egypt, not God! No wonder this indictment sounds a contemptuous note. Psalm 2:1-5 is similar, portraying God as laughing at the nations which conspire against Him. Isaiah 40 continues the theme, remarking that humanity is "a drop in a bucket" (vs. 15), "dust on the scales" (vs. 15) and "like grasshoppers" (vs. 22). The truth is driven home in Isaiah 40:25: " 'To whom will you compare me? Or who is my equal?' says the Holy One."

God's Promise (31:4, 5)

31:4 God often uses similes to communicate His nature to His people. But since no one picture is complete; many similes must be used. Our concept of God becomes more complete as we allow additional pictures to sharpen that concept.

Two powerful images are presented in these verses. The first is that of "a great lion over his prey" (vs. 4). Just as a hungry lion will not be frightened by the shouts of the shepherds into releasing the lamb or sheep it has in its jaws, so God's judgment cannot be averted by the mere military might of the Egyptians. God will come down as "the Lord Almighty" to "do battle on Mount Zion and on its heights." The Lord will fight against the wicked of Judah, permitting His own army to march on and to destroy the city despite any help that the Egyptians could offer.

31:5 The second image is one of protection and comfort. When their nests are threatened, some birds flutter or hover above their young ones to shield them from the eyes of predators. God will protect Jerusalem with the same loving care. The analogy of a mother bird is one that David also enjoyed using: "Because you are my help, I sing in the shadow of your wings" (Ps. 63:7). The lion-like fierceness of God takes the form of a mother bird's protective care. Even though the physical city of Jerusalem will be destroyed, God will show mercy toward a remnant. The judgment won't mean the end of His people. God has promised to protect, preserve and plan for His people's future.

God's Plea (31:6, 7)

31:6 "Return to him you have so greatly revolted against," Isaiah cries. Repent, turn back to God. Even though God had declared that the nation would not repent and would be carried into exile, it still would not perish completely. God would bless it so that the true children of Israel would return to God. His motive all along has been to drive His people back to Himself. He gets no thrill out of punishing His people, but it seems to be the only thing that will make them turn back to Him.

"O Israelites" reminds the listeners who they are—the chosen people of God. Don't forget your heritage, Isaiah is saying. But to be the true Israelites, they must abandon their course of deep rebellion and turn back to God. "Let the sons of Israel do as Israel himself had done," says Young. "Let them cease being Jacob and become Israel; let them return unto the Lord."

This prophecy was given in the midst of a period of national repentance and reform. But Hezekiah's reign marked only a temporary return—a godly interval between Ahaz and Manasseh. God's pronouncement of judgment showed He knew the people's repentance was temporary.

31:7 "In that day" refers to the time when God finally will deliver His people. When the people see the folly of their ways, they "will reject the idols of silver and gold [their] sinful hands have made." The phrasing points out double foolishness: confidence in idols and confidence in the human hands that made them. You will see how foolish you have been, the prophet seems to be saying, how doubly foolish.

God's Pronouncement (31:8, 9)

31:8 "Assyria will fall by a sword that is not of man" reflects God's indictment against this powerful nation. Her fall will be so complete that "their young men will be put to forced labor." Even in Judah's lowest moments, when she was paying tribute to Assyria, her young men were not part of that tribute. Assyria would pay the heaviest tribute possible with the lives of the young men able to fight her battles.

31:9 Such power—God's power—will so overtake the warriors of Assyria that they will panic and run. The refuge they found among the rocks and crevices will be worthless. The Lord is the one who declares these things, says Isaiah. The Lord has a "fire in Zion," the continual fire on the altar of burnt offering. He also has a "furnace in Jerusalem," reflecting His wrath, which is ready to consume His enemies.

For Discussion

1. What is God suggesting about the character of the Israelites in verse 1? The Israelites may have felt that they were "hedging their bets," relying on the Egyptians "just in case." How do you think God views this attitude?

2. How does God say He compares with the Egyptians? Why do you think he thought it necessary to draw this distinction? Under what circumstances might you find verse 3 an encouragement?

3. How were the Israelites doubly foolish? Are there ways in which overconfidence in yourself and in something you have done has reflected double foolishness? Discuss.

Window on the Word

Self-centered!

Theodore Roosevelt, sometimes known as Roosevelt the First, was a president who thought he knew his value.

"Father always had to be the center of attention," said one of his children. "When he went to a wedding, he wanted to be the bride. When he went to a funeral, he was sorry that he couldn't be the corpse." *(Signs of the Times)*

5

A Day of Gladness And Joy

Truth to Apply: The transformation I experienced when I became a Christian brought a joy I need to share with others.

Key Verse: And the ransomed of the Lord will return. They will enter Zion with singing; everlasting joy will crown their heads. Gladness and joy will overtake them, and sorrow and sighing will flee away (Isa. 35:10).

Mother Teresa was awarded the 1979 Nobel Peace Prize for her work among lepers and the poorest of the poor in India. She once spoke to an itinerant drama troupe called "Chant of Asia" about the joy of serving: "We give joy to people by serving them; you, you give it by your performance. Your work and ours complete each other. What you do by singing and dancing, we do by scrubbing and cleaning. It is beautiful to give joy to people. I am sure that thanks to you many people are comforted. And this talent you have received, only riches can deprive you of it. As long as you are willing to be empty of yourself and to be filled with God, you will keep this talent. The day that we begin to grow rich we lose something and begin to die.

" . . . We serve the same Lord. All over the globe, people hunger and thirst for God's love. In your way, you satisfy this hunger by spreading joy. In our way, we give joy by putting ourselves at the service of the sick, the dying, the rejected" (Mother Teresa, *The Love of Christ*, Harper & Row, 1982).

What forms of service can result in people receiving the joy of Christ? Why is it important for you to find the ways that you are best able to share your joy in Christ? Share your insights about what some of these ways might be.

Background/Overview: *Isaiah 35:1-10*

After the Israelites crossed the Red Sea in their flight from Egypt, they came to the Desert of Shur and traveled for three days without finding water (Ex. 15:22). Not far beyond Shur the Lord sweetened the bitter waters of Marah (Ex. 15:24, 25).

Another time, they camped at Rephidim, "but there was no water for the people to drink" (Ex. 17:1). So the Lord told Moses, "Strike the rock, and water will come out of it for the people to drink" (Ex. 17:6).

The ancient Hebrews thought of the sea as life threatening, a symbol of chaos. But from their years of wandering in the desert, they should have altered that view to see the life-giving nature of fresh water, rivers and springs. Fresh water made life possible. The flowing springs were a gift of God's creation. God's people then could understand how the God who satisfied their physical needs was also able to satisfy their spiritual needs.

God's provision of water in the desert was remembered in the context of acknowledging the Lordship of Yahweh and his continuing acts of salvation on their behalf. Water also came to be associated, not just with past and present salvation, but with future salvation.

In the coming reign of peace, the prophets of Israel anticipated an abundance of thirst-quenching water. Against this backdrop we come to Isaiah 35, where God's salvation is portrayed as "streams in the desert . . . bubbling springs" (35:6, 7).

Light on the Text

The Desert Transformed (35:1, 2)

35:1 In chapter 34, Isaiah pronounces the Lord's judgment against the nation. The speech is laden with blood, vengeance, and retribution. In contrast, chapter 35 sings the joyous transformation that will occur when God redeems His people. "The desert and the parched land will be glad . . . the wilderness will rejoice and blossom." This timbre characterizes the rest of the chapter.

35:2 A complete reversal is to take place. The desert, defined by its sun, scorched earth and scarce foliage, will blossom. "Like the crocus," which peeks its head through the earth in the early spring, "it will burst into bloom." "Aha! The 'glory of the Lord' is here," it will cry. "I see 'the splendor of our God!' "

"The glory of Lebanon will be given to it" refers to the beautiful trees and magnificent vegetation that made Lebanon famous. Carmel, the area around Mount Carmel, was famed in Palestine for its beauty. Sharon is the fertile coastal plain below Mount Carmel. The desert will be like these areas, Isaiah says. That seemingly impossible transformation symbolizes what happens when God's grace is introduced to the desert heart.

The Heart Transformed (35:3, 4)

Judah was about to fall in a heap of despair. The prophet comes with a message of hope: "Be strong, do not fear; your God will come" (vs. 4). With this message, he says (vs. 3), "Strengthen the feeble hands," so they are able to finish their task; "steady the knees that give way," so they may continue the journey; speak to "fearful hearts," so they do not give up. Nothing in their circumstances may have immediately changed, but their outlook was to be transformed by the hope they received. God was coming with "vengeance; with divine retribution" (vs. 4) on the enemies of God's people. These are the very words used to describe the punishment of the nations who oppose God in chapter 34, a judgment that would create deserts (34:8-11). Here, God promises a restoration of the land as the result of His grace. "He will come to save you," rather than destroy Israel as He had promised to destroy Edom.

Creation Transformed (35:5-7)

35:5, 6 When God comes with His salvation, the world system will be changed. This occurred in part during Jesus'ministry, as He declared His purpose, quoting from

Isaiah 61:1, 2: "The Spirit of the Lord is on me, because he has anointed me to preach good news to the poor. He has sent me to proclaim freedom for the prisoners and recovery of sight for the blind, to release the oppressed, to proclaim the year of the Lord's favor" (Lk. 4:18, 19). When the Lord returns, He will bring with Him a radical change in the world, just as when the Messiah came, He brought the beginnings of that transformation.

The prophet provides a list of changes: "Then will the eyes of the blind be opened and the ears of the deaf unstopped" (vs. 5). Not only will the lame walk, they will "leap like a deer"; not only will the mute speak, they will "shout for joy" (vs. 6). Where there was wilderness, "water will gush forth."

35:7 Isaiah goes on to detail the changes from desert life to life with ample water supplies. Where there was once "burning sand," there will be pools of water, bubbling springs, running water. The very hideouts of the carniverous, conniving jackal will be the home of marsh vegetation—"grass and reeds and papyrus."

A Highway of Transformation (35:8-10)

35:8 The climax of the poem uses the image of the highway upon which the redeemed of the Lord will travel. "The Way of Holiness" is a road running through the desert and transforming it. It is a private road, reserved only for those who have been cleansed and purified by God. The way is holy, however, not because of some intrinsic quality in the road but because of the character of those who walk there. "Wicked fools will not go about on it" is the same sense as "the unclean will not journey on it." One might very easily lose her way in a desert crossing. Sand may blow across the path; the road itself may not have been well-defined in the first place. But the one who walks on the Way of Holiness has a sure, certain road.

35:9 The Way of Holiness is a road free of danger. Though it may pass through regions where wildlife abounds, "no lion will be there, nor will any ferocious beast get up on it." The usual dangers to the traveler simply will not be threats to those journeying on the holy road.

Who will travel on the road? The poem reiterates, "only the redeemed will walk there." Only the rightful heirs of the promises of God will walk in the Way of Holiness, those who have been delivered out of the hands of the enemy. The prophet refers not just to a physical deliverance, though that certainly would have been important to people living in physical captivity, but also to a spiritual deliverance.

35:10 "The ransomed of the Lord will return" sums up the rich promises of restoration and renewal. Those who have been far from Zion will return to the Holy City with singing, with "everlasting joy," a joy that overcomes sorrow and sighing. This is a day to look forward to: when the people of God are freed from their sins, when they return to the city of God to live with Him, when the heaviness of "sorrow and sighing will flee away," replaced with "gladness and joy."

For Discussion

1. What are the changes that are to occur in the desert? Was the prophet referring to the desert areas of Judah and Israel? Might he also have been referring to the deserts in human hearts?

2. How does the poem reflect the changes that are to occur in human hearts? Is this transformation what happens when one becomes a Christian, or is it a continuing renewal and change?

3. What is your reaction to the statement that God will come with vengeance and divine retribution? How do these characteristics mesh with His love and mercy?

4. What demeanor characterizes those who walk in the Way of Holiness? If you think you are walking on it now, do you possess those elements of joy and gladness? Are there ways in which gladness and joy overcome sorrow and sighing now, even though the burdens of this world are not entirely done away with? Why might this

viewpoint give you hope? What is the future hope that is part of this prophecy?

Window on the Word

Transformaion Takes Time

"What is REAL?" asked the Rabbit one day, when they were lying side by side near the nursery fender, before Nana came to tidy the room. "Does it mean having things that buzz inside you and a stick-out handle?"

"Real isn't how you are made," said the Skin Horse. "It's a thing that happens to you. When a child loves you for a long, long time, not just to play with, but REALLY loves you, then you become Real."

"Does it hurt?" asked the Rabbit.

"'Sometimes," said the Skin Horse, for he was always truthful. "When you are Real you don't mind being hurt."

"Does it happen all at once, like being wound up," he asked, "or bit by bit?"

"It doesn't happen all at once," said the Skin Horse. "You become. It takes a long time. That's why it doesn't often happen to people who break easily, or have sharp edges, or who have to be carefully kept. Generally, by the time you are Real, most of your hair has been loved off, and your eyes drop out and you get loose in the joints and very shabby. But these things don't matter at all, because once you are Real you can't be ugly, except to people who don't understand."

(Margery Williams, *The Velveteen Rabbit*, Doubleday)

6

I Am the Lord

Truth to Apply: God's promises to protect Israel are also His promises to protect me.

Key Verse: Turn to me and be saved, all you ends of the earth; for I am God, and there is no other (Isa. 45:22).

At Christmastime, a friend bought something for me, and I reached for a check to repay him the ten dollars and fifty cents. Because I have both French Huguenot and Scots' blood I am stubborn and frugal: I saw no reason why my old checks weren't still valid, and I wasn't about to waste them.

My friend said, "Oh, come off it, Madeleine, you know that check won't go through."

I asked, "Do you really and truly mean that my signature, my name, means nothing, absolutely nothing at all?"

"That's what I mean. . . . "

"All right, then, I feel like Emily Bronte today," and signed [the check] . . . Emily Bronte. . . .

"You just told me that my name means nothing, absolutely nothing at all. Okay, so I feel like Emily Bronte and I don't see why I shouldn't sign it Emily Bronte. Take it—just for fun—and let's see what happens . . . . If it bounces I'll write you another check."

It did not bounce. I now have cancelled checks signed Emily Bronte, Jane Austen, and Elizabeth Barrett Browning (Madeleine L'Engle, *A Circle of Quiet*, Seabury, 1979).

What does L'Engle's experience indicate about our society? Why are names important? What does your name say about you? In what ways do the names of God give you a sense of being cared for and protected?

Background/Overview: *Isaiah 43:1-7*

Isaiah 43:1-7 may be the last half of a poem that begins with Isaiah 42:18. According to one arrangement, it is the fifth in a series of poems that opens the second half of Isaiah. Each of these poems ends on a positive note of promise and hope.

The first poem concludes with the words, "He tends his flock like a shephered: He gathers the lambs in his arms and carries them close to his heart; he gently leads those that have young" (Isa. 40:11). The second poem concludes with the familiar words, "but those who hope in the Lord will renew their strength. They will soar on wings like eagles; they will run and not grow weary, they will walk and not be faint" (Isa. 40:31).

The poem in this lesson speaks of Israel in terms of a deaf and blind servant (42:18-20). The people are described as "plundered and looted" (42:22), the country in shambles (42:25). After all this, however, God will gather His people around Him, calling them by His name (43:6, 7).

With this lesson we begin study in the second half of the Book of Isaiah, which has traditionally been divided into two parts: chapters 1—39, Themes of Fruitfulness and Commitment; and chapters 40—66, Themes of Comfort and Hope. Aptly called "The Book of Comfort," the second half of Isaiah is characterized by its opening: "Comfort, comfort my people, says your God" (40:1). The poems that begin this section fulfill that requirement; herein lies great comfort, great love and tenderness for the wounded people of God.

Light on the Text

God Restores and Redeems (43:1)

The first half of this poem, Isaiah 42:18-25, ends with a grim picture of the Lord's anger: "It [His anger] enveloped them in flames . . . it consumed them . . . " (42:25). The Israelites have been "plundered and looted

. . . hidden away in prisons" (42:22). And the Lord is the one who handed them over (42:24).

"But now" (43:1) a change is to take place. The dismal condition of the people will be replaced with the glorious redemption of God. Israel's experience in Egypt comes to mind, when they were in daily misery under the hand of Pharaoh. But God sent them Moses, who led them out of slavery into freedom. They soon forgot all that, however, and their disobedience led to exile in Babylon, a captivity not unlike that in Egypt.

Who is going to cause the change? The same One who handed Jacob and Israel over to become looted and plundered is "he who created you, O Jacob, he who formed you, O Israel." The people are reminded to whom they owe their existence. The development of Israel as a nation was so remarkable that the prophet likens it to the original Creation. God created Israel out of nothing. No other nation was a distinctive theocracy.

Isaiah uses this double designation of "Jacob and Israel" many times in chapters 40-49. "Jacob was the deceiver and had to become Israel," notes Young. " . . . There may be a hint that the Jacob character of the nation had to be abandoned. Implied also may be the thought that in 'Israel' is expressed the true destiny of the people."

"Fear not" indicates that, though the people will not be immune from suffering, neither have things gone out of control. God's redemption was not exhausted in the flight from Egypt, nor would it be exhausted in the return from exile in Babylon. God will continue to save His people, "to buy [them] out of slavery," as the word "redemption" indicates. His salvation would be fully expressed in the redemption provided by the Messiah.

By noting their origins—in their father Jacob/Israel—God points out that he has called them by name, summoning them to be His and to serve Him. This is similar to the way a shepherd calls his sheep by name, because they are his and he knows them well.

God Loves and Protects (43:2-4)

43:2 Still, the redeemed must pass through great trials. Water and fire embody the elements of judgment; they are also the elements of purification. God judged the earth with a flood in Noah's day; He would finally judge the earth with fire. The verse does not reflect just the future, final judgment but says, "when you pass through . . . ," that is, "whenever." Though the water covered the earth in Noah's day, he and his family were saved. Though the Israelites passed through the river when they fled Egypt, it did not sweep over them. Though the fires of judgment would destroy the earth, God's people would not be burned.

43:3 God names Himself three times here: "I am the Lord, your God," Yahweh, who entered into a covenant with them at Sinai and delivered them from slavery in Egypt. He is the same Lord, and He still acts in their behalf. "I am . . . the Holy One of Israel," in contrast to the many gods of the heathen. The Holy One has a special concern for His people; the gods of the heathen were selfish and demanding, concerned only for themselves. "I am . . . your Savior," the One who saves. The thought in the latter part of this verse, "I give Egypt for your ransom, Cush and Seba in your stead," is that God rewarded Persia for releasing the Jewish captives by enabling Persia to conquer Egypt, Cush (contemporary southern Egypt, Sudan, northern Ethiopia) and Seba (possible Sheba in southern Arabia).

43:4 "Since you are precious and honored in my sight" may be read "Due to the fact that I have singled you out as valuable." Furthermore, God loves them. Due to these facts, He reiterates, other people will receive the calamities of war in their stead.

How Does God Protect Us?

The question of God's protecting presence must always be asked against the background of His broader purpose for humankind, and for each of us in particular. That is, we should ask about God's protection in the light of His will for us. After all, the Father seemed to withdraw Himself from the Son at His darkest hour, on the cross. Yet, in reality, the darkness the Son experienced then was a prelude to a perfection of knowledge, not the darkness of utter abandonment.

The protection we are offered as Christians is the protection of God's loving hand. Nothing can snatch us out of security—not physical pain, not mental anguish, not economic depression. After all, we are more than our bodies or our minds. We do not live by bread alone. We have received a new life from God and it is this life that He nurtures and protects.

In a real sense, we live in two worlds: in this space-time continuum, and in the Kingdom of God. And sometimes it happens that the life in the one must suffer that the greater Life in the other may grow and flourish.

God Gathers and Names (43:5-7)

43:5 The second half of the prophet's poem on God's redeeming love comes to a fitting climax with repetition of the comforting words, "Do not be afraid, for I am with you . . . ." These were assurances the exiles would be comforted to hear.

Though we often think of the Babylonian Captivity as a movement of the Israelites en masse from Israel to Babylon, the Babylonian Empire was vast. The Israelites, therefore, were widely scattered. It was truly a *diaspora,* an extensive dispersal of the people of God.

43:6 This prophetic poem was intended to reassure the Israelites that though the time was coming when they would be scattered in all directions, eventually they would be brought back home again. "I will bring your children from the east and gather you from the west. I will say to the north, 'Give them up!' and to the south, 'Do not hold them back.' Bring my sons from afar and my daughters from the ends of the earth."

There is deeper significance to this beautiful passage of Scripture. It suggests the time when the spiritual sons and daughters of Abraham will be restored to God the Father by the blood of Christ, "from every tribe and language and people and nation" (Rev. 5:9).

43:7 The people of Israel would be called by God's name, the name that He gave to them. This is a clear identification of the ones whom God will bring back to Himself. It further indicates that not all who called themselves

Israelites also bore the name of God.

The second part of the verse, "whom I created for my glory," explains why God "formed and made" Israel in the first place. More than once, Moses reminded God that if He destroyed the rebellious Hebrews, God's name would be blemished, for He purposed to demonstrate His greatness through them. Part of God's reasoning for restoring His people, then, was to display His glory in His care of them.

For Discussion

1. Why were the Israelites not to be afraid? What credentials does God give for being qualified to redeem Israel? Why was it important that the Israelites be called by name? By whose name were they called? Why is your name important? Do you also call yourself "Christian"?

2. What were the waters and fire that the Israelites had gone through or were about to go through? Have you gone through water? Did you drown? Were there times when you thought you might? Have you gone through fire? Did you burn up? Did you "feel the heat"? How so?

3. What did God do to show that the Israelites were "precious and honored" in His sight? How has He demonstrated to you that you are special? How is His love for believers different from His love for humanity in general?

4. What does God promise to do for the children of Israel (v.6)? How will this group of people be different from the children of Israel of Isaiah's day? By whose name will they be called? Are you called by that name? Then are you one of those who will be gathered "from the ends of the earth"?

5. Why did God create a people for Himself? What difference does it make that God wants to show His glory through His people? What difference should it make in how you act?

I'm Talking to You

In Handel's *Messiah,* the composer treats Isaiah 40:1-11 much like the prophet does. The first three verses are a recitative, spoken almost tentatively. In the fourth verse, a solo voice calmly announces that "Every valley shall be raised up, every mountain and hill made low." And then the fifth verse explodes with the chorus singing that "the glory of the Lord will be revealed, and all mankind together will see it." A sequence of scenes comes to mind. The angels are proclaiming the glory of the Lord, lighting up the heavens with the glory with which God has clothed them. A farmer in Iowa emerges from the darkness of his barn to take a look. Factory workers in Newark crowd at the door to see what's happening. A young couple in south Philly stop their quarrel in mid-sentence and go to the door. All the world pauses, and turns.

Like a mother takes the chin of her child in her hand and turns the child's face to her and says, "Listen, child, I'm talking to you," God takes the faces of all His Creation in His hand and says, "Listen, this is very important. I'm talking to you." It is a huge picture, earth suspended in space, God's hands encompassing His Creation.

Then the contrast, sung in lilting, tender tones in *Messiah:* "He tends his flock like a shepherd: he gathers the lambs in his arms and carries them close to his heart; he gently leads those that have young." It is spring. There are newborn lambs, and there are mothers staggering under the weight of their unborn babies. The shepherd leads his flock slowly, ever so slowly. But then, there is no hurry. They must find more pasture, but because it is spring, grass is bountiful and they don't have to move far. So the lambs lolligag, they romp, they hassle their moms. The shepherd laughs and gathers a lamb in his arms, not just kissing a wet nose and putting her down, but holding her close to his heart, scratching her behind the ears and talking to her.

We anticipate the moment when the immense God of

all Creation and the intimate God of His people are presented to us in a way we can understand. Thus He was presented, as recorded in Luke 2:8-14. There were, as the writer of Hebrews puts it, "thousands upon thousands of angels in joyful assembly," worshipping God the Creator, God the Magnificent, God the Overwhelming. And to whom did the angels come? They came to shepherds, caretakers of the helpless.

So the shepherds went to Bethlehem to see this thing that had happened, which the Lord had told them about. They crept into the stable, trying not to wake the child or his exhausted mother. And one of them, the one with five kids and another on the way, the one with hands so roughened by the weather that the callouses were permanently stained with dirt, the one with a deep gash across the back of one of his hands where he'd freed a lamb caught in a thornbush—that one knelt right next to the manger-become-crib. That one took a tiny chin in his hand and turned the child's face to him. That common hand held an uncommon face, and the world paused, because the glory of the Lord was revealed. That is the moment for which we wait!

(Advent devotional by Yvonne R. Schultz)

7

The Servant of the Lord

Truth to Apply: Jesus, the Suffering Servant, bore my sins so I might live in His light.

Key Verse: Here is my servant, whom I uphold, my chosen one in whom I delight; I will put my Spirit on him and he will bring justice to the nations (Isa. 42:1).

Little lamb, who made thee?
Dost thou know who made thee?
Gave thee life, and bid thee feed
By the stream and o'er the mead;
Gave thee clothing of delight,
Softest clothing, woolly, bright;
Gave thee such a tender voice,
Making all the vales rejoice?

Little lamb, who made thee?
Dost thou know who made thee?
Little lamb, I'll tell thee,
Little lamb, I'll tell thee:

He is called by thy name,
For He calls Himself a Lamb.
He is meek, and He is mild;
He became a little child.

I a child, and thou a lamb.
We are called by His name.
Little lamb, God bless thee!
Little lamb, God bless thee!"

"The Lamb" by William Blake (*Songs of Innocence*) takes us back to the source of the simile, "He was led like a lamb to the slaughter, and as a sheep before her shearers is silent, so he did not open his mouth" (Isa. 53:7). How does Blake say Jesus was like a lamb? How are we like sheep?

Background/Overview: *Isaiah 42:1-4; 53:4-6*

Chapters 40—66 of Isaiah form a collection of poems of supreme literary quality, which the prophet may have recited for various occasions. Among these poems are several songs about a servant whom God would send to save His people. The passages for this lesson's study are taken from those "Servant Songs."

The theme of the Servant of the Lord is common throughout Isaiah 40-66. It appears in one section as a reference to a conqueror from the East whom God would send to liberate Israel from Babylonian exile (Isa. 44:28; 45:1). Cyrus, the Persian emperor, is this servant. Though Cyrus did not acknowledge God as his Lord (45:4), he did God's will.

God also calls the nation of Israel a servant (Isa. 41:8-10; 44:1,2). She was chosen by God to live in a special relationship to Him. Through her, God's work of redemption was to be accomplished. Regretfully, however, Israel neglected this calling, instead often indulging in idolatry and immorality.

Spiritual redemption was to be accomplished by another Servant, unnamed, but clearly the Messiah. Isaiah earlier referred to Him in chapter 11. This servant, Jesus, will do what Cyrus could not; and he will serve as Israel failed to do.

Light on the Text

Here Is My Servant (42:1-4)

42:1, 2 "Here is my servant," the prophet begins. Sit up and take notice, because I have someone important for you to meet. Who is he? This and the following verses suggest that the servant is the Messiah. In Isaiah 44:1, the audience is identified as " . . . Jacob, my servant, Israel, whom I have chosen," a clear identification of God's people, the nation of Israel, but here the reference is to an individual, "my chosen one." He who is the servant is also the one in whom God delights. The statement of relationship this early in the passage is significant, for it sets the tone for all the Servant Songs: He is a servant, as is a slave; he is chosen, as is a son.

God promises to "uphold" His servant, to sustain him. He will do this by putting His Spirit on him, by giving the servant the power to do God's will. With the Spirit comes not only power, but authority to "proclaim justice to the nations." Matthew 12:18b, another rendering of this passage, says "he will proclaim justice to the nations." The verb does not mean "to call" or "to proclaim," but "to cause to go out." The Messiah, then, will announce justice, preaching it to the people, but by the authority given Him by the Holy Spirit, He will also cause it to be spread throughout the world.

By using negative verbs, verse 2 contrasts the working of the servant to the way a worldly conqueror operates: "He will not shout or cry out, or raise his voice in the streets." When a conqueror took possession of a nation, one of the first things he did was to introduce his own religion. This he did by having orders for submission shouted in the streets, by forcing his god on the people. The phrase "He will not . . . cry out" may refer to the constant rebuke to which a king would subject his population, much as Cyrus did. This the Messiah would not do. The Messiah's difficult mission will succeed, but not by force. His teaching will be done not by loud proclamation, but by quiet instruction to a handful of men and women.

42:3 Symbolic figures of the weak and oppressed dominate verse 3. "A bruised reed" is a weak marsh plant, delicate when it is healthy, easily destroyed when bent or bruised by the wind or by a clumsy creature crawling through the swamp. Likewise, the "smoldering wick" is about to go out. A strong flame is easily extinguished, but a smoldering wick is even more fragile. Who are these people? They are those who are bruised, bent over by the winds of life, perhaps even by the simple drudgeries of life. Those who were oppressed by a foreign ruler may have despaired to the point of feeling as if they would be snuffed out ("How can we sing the songs of the

Lord while in a foreign land?" asked the Psalmist [137:4]). The servant would not break or snuff out the weak and oppressed, but salve their wounds and restore their strength.

42:4 Unlike the bruised reed and the smoldering wick, the servant "will not falter or be discouraged." Though His mission is a difficult one, He will be faithful to His task, which is to establish justice on earth. This points to the universality of His work. "The conversion of the heathen," writes Young, "is not the result of one mighty, eschatological act, but of the gradual, tireless work of the servant." The phrasing indicates that one way the Messiah will bring forth and establish justice is to bring forth and establish His servants, God's people, on earth. Like the Servant, the servants will be given the power and authority to "not falter or be discouraged" until their task is completed.

The Peace of God (53:4-6)

53:4 Isaiah 53 is one of the most beloved passages of the Bible, for it describes the immensity of the sacrificial work of Christ. The Messiah's death on the cross was not a simple death, for even in His arrest, trial, punishment and path to the cross, He conducted Himself as the Lamb of God.

The poem begins in Isaiah 52:13 and continues through the end of chapter 53. It depicts the Suffering Servant in a way that must have jarred those who heard Isaiah's prophecy. Rather than being recognized as king, the Servant is "despised and rejected by men" (53:3). But in the following verses, the prophet shows us that the Servant's suffering was actually the heart of His mission. In His death, He won a victory.

The Servant is "a man of sorrows, and familiar with suffering," but they are not His own sorrows. "Surely he took up our infirmities and carried our sorrows," verse 4 begins. The nature of the atonement is introduced with the fact that Christ's death was a substitute for our deaths. Our sorrows and sufferings were placed on Christ as a substitute for us. He lifted up and carried them, instead of us lifting and carrying them.

Instead of us understanding what He did, however, we thought He was being "stricken by God, smitten by him, and afflicted," as with a dread disease. God must be punishing Him for something He did, we thought, much like Job's family and friends thought He was being punished for something He did. How ironic that the nature of the affliction Christ accepted was reflective of the nature of the sins He carried for us.

53:5 Strong, vivid words mark verse 5: "pierced," "crushed," "punishment," "wounds." The servant will be in such a condition "for our transgressions," that is, because we have sinned. As the lamb's throat was slit for sacrifice, the Lamb of God would be pierced—His hands and feet nailed to the cross, and His side cut open. The lamb in the old sacrificial system was a substitute for the sins of the people; so the Lamb of God would be a substitute for the sins of the people. As the lamb was totally destroyed, so the Lamb of God would be "crushed for our iniquities." Our iniquities are not merely the breaking of human laws, but a rebellion against the Law of God, His Word.

The violent, warlike nature of Christ's death is compared with the result—our peace. This is the *shalom* of God, the peace that God maintains toward His people. The word involves more than a sense of well-being, more than a lack of conflict. It is a virtue, a blessing, the fulfillment of a deep need. "If 'peace' refers only to well-being or to material prosperity," says Young, "it is difficult to perceive why the death of the servant was necessary to procure that peace." Rather, this peace is the peace of God that passes understanding.

The severity of His wounds, of His punishment, is compared with the result—our healing. For us, there is freedom from what caused the servant to die. No longer need we suffer from spiritual wounds, the sins and rebellion that separate us from God. Though remnants of sin will continue to plague us, the promise of full and final redemption is included in the atonement. Emotional wounds, the anger and hatred that others inflict on us, no longer need to dominate us. Though we may not be able to forget or to stop feeling some of the pain, there is restoration and healing in Christ's pain. No longer need we be overcome by physical infirmities, whether chronic illness or the weariness of life. For though we continue to experience our physical inadequacies, the healing of the Cross provides hope and comfort.

53:6 "We all . . . " begins verse 6, and it concludes the same way: " . . . us all." All of us have gone astray, like sheep without a shepherd. Those who are familiar with sheep are impressed by the stupidity and utter helplessness of these animals. By using the image of sheep, God tells us much about ourselves, and much about Himself as the Shepherd.

Like sheep, we become easily lost, paralyzed with fear when we do. Like sheep, we follow each other without considering where we may end up. Like sheep, we are easy prey for wolves and other carnivorous animals.

The effect of our straying, however, is not borne by us, but was borne by Christ: "The Lord has laid on him the iniquity of us all." Jesus was our representative, the Lamb among lambs, the one substitute for the sins of us all.

For Discussion

1. What are the characteristics of the servant? What qualities marked Jesus' ministry? How was His leadership exercised differently from Cyrus's? How is Christ's servanthood/leadership in His church exercised today? How is His servanthood/leadership exercised by you at home? at work? What does this tell you about your church leaders? yourself?

2. What is the "bruised reed" and "smoldering wick" referred to in 42:3? Do you know someone who seemed about to break whom God restored? Do you know someone, who seemed about to give up, whom God gave new strength? How have you been in that situation? What did Christ do for you?

3. What does Isaiah 53:4 say the servant did? How did we regard Him for having done this? What do you tend

to think when someone seems to have one calamity after another? In light of this passage, how shall we view this person?

4. How does Isaiah 53:4-6 match the account (Mt. 27:11-55) of the sufferings of Christ as He was led to crucifixion? What do His physical sufferings have to do with our sins? What do you think is the relationship between Christ's physical suffering and our physical suffering? What do you think is being promised in these verses about healing?

5. How are we like sheep? Review from Isaiah 40:11 how Jesus is like a shepherd. What does this say about how church leaders are to be shepherds (see I Pet. 5:2-4)?

6. What was the final act of Jesus' servanthood? Do you think we are expected to follow His example of giving His life for His sheep? How do you give your life for the well-being of others in the flock of God? What more might you do as a result of studying these verses?

Window on the Word

The Story As It Was Meant to Be

The mythological Phoenix finds a creative context in *Potter*, by Walter Wangerin, Jr. (Chariot, 1985). It is the story of a boy who learns to accept the death of his best friend by witnessing the death of the Phoenix. In this story, we may see the splendor of the sufferings of Christ, who died for us:

"The Phoenix began to sing.

"Dear God, what a song that was! As though his throat were the pipe of an organ, he made the air to tremble with deep music, woeful majesty at the mouth of the Phoenix and trumpets of supplication. He played pathetic melodies among the baritones, for his memory was long and grievous. Oboes wept and the flutes accused. What did the Phoneix sing? He sang five hundred years of wars. . . . The Phoenix sang of the sorrow of men, of the fightings and dyings in half one thousand years, and his song was grand, and his song was sad at once.

" . . . But then the Phoenix himself gave up the song, too terrible to bear, and bowed his head. Silence. In that moment the sun loosed his reins. The horses felt the slack and bounded up with a greater speed. Their hooves struck sparks from the firmament. The sparks rained burning upon the earth, and they caught in the nest of the Phoenix, and the nest burst into flame. The Phoenix did not so much as raise his head; he seemed to know that this would be the result of his song, and maybe it was the purpose. A sweet, blue fire hissed in the spices beneath him. Smoke closed over him. But the Phoenix kept his head bowed down and did not move.

" . . . His own bright feathers caught fire. His tail became a torch and his wings spread out spilling flames, and he laid his head across the coals and allowed himself to be swallowed in the burning.

"And he died.

"Poor Potter sobbed and sobbed.

" . . . 'Hush, Potter,' said the Oriole. 'This is the story. This is the way that it is supposed to be.'

" 'But I loved him,' Potter wept.

" 'And he loved you,' said the Oriole.

" 'Oh, Baltimore Oriole, Phoenix didn't even know me.'

" 'Yes, he did. By name,' said the Oriole."

8

Come to the Feast

Truth to Apply: My hunger and thirst for God is satisfied as I turn to God's Word.

Key Verse: Seek the Lord while he may be found; call on him while he is near (Isa. 55:6).

Margaret Clarkson describes the first time she found a natural spring of water. She had been taken by an aunt to a cottage in the highlands. Their food had to come from a village five miles away, to which they had to walk.

"It was in that village that I first discovered water—cold, clear, and delicious—flowing from a crevice in a great rock jutting from a wooded hillside. Oh, the joy of skipping into the cool dimness after the long, hot trudge to town, and drinking of that never-to-be-forgotten water from the rock! Decades later, I can feel the excitement and magic of that still green glade, and taste again that sparkling spring water.

"Since then I have found many a bubbling spring while wandering in field and woodland, but I have never got over the wonder of drinking water in the wilderness, fresh from the hand of God.

"Yet I have drunk of these lovely waters only to thirst again. Jesus gives living waters of which thirsty souls may drink and never thirst again. He bids all who desire it to take freely of the water of life. And that water is Christ himself, a well of water springing up unto everlasting life" (*All Nature Sings,* Wm. B. Eerdmans, 1986).

Can you remember the time you were thirstier than you had ever been before or have been since? What was it like? What did you do to appease your thirst?

Background/Overview: *Isaiah 55:1-11*

God's patience had run out with Israel, as a people and a political power. Just as God judged the Northern Kingdom by allowing Assyria to conquer it, now the Southern Kingdom faced devastation by the Babylonians.

So certain was this prophecy of judgment that Isaiah devoted much of his written work to comforting the nation in exile (Isa. 40—66). He included the announcement that deliverance was coming and that God had not forgotten His people.

The fate of the Jews in captivity could have been worse. Rather than being treated as prisoners of war or as slaves, they were, for the most part, resettled as free persons. Many of the exiles achieved a relatively high degree of economic success. Because of Babylon's custom of using members of conquered peoples to staff high governmental offices, some Hebrews, such as Daniel, even attained high political status.

Still, the thirst of a person's soul cannot be quenched by fame or fortune. The Jews were never able to forget their homeland or the promises God had made to them in regard to their homeland.

But how could the captive Jew return to his homeland to serve God? From a human standpoint, it was impossible. The Babylonians would prevent it. God's methods, however, are not thwarted by human circumstances.

The firm promise of God was that the Israelites would be redeemed from Babylon, even though it seemed impossible. They would "go out in joy and be led forth in peace" (Isa. 55:12). In the passages under consideration, we see how God promised joy and satisfaction even more complete than that offered by release from Babylonian Captivity.

Light on the Text

Invitation to the Thirsty (55:1-3)

55:1 As a vendor in the street, hawking water, the prophet cries out for participants in the feast of God: "Come"! Everything is ready! All the guests are invited. Nothing is asked of them except to come. There is also in the cry a note of compassion, perhaps even of pity, because those who are invited are dying of hunger and thirst. They may be dressed in the finest clothing, live in the choicest suburbs, own the latest technology, vacation in the hottest spots, but they lack the essential elements of a satisfying life—the water, wine, milk, bread, "the richest of fare" of the Holy Spirit. The imperatives stress the legitimacy of the invitation: "Come . . . come, buy . . . ."

But how can one "buy wine and milk without money and without cost"? The language points out that the water, wine, and milk are not available for purchase with dollars, but by divine grace. Note that a transaction has occurred, however. This feast didn't magically appear; it was bought with the sacrifice of the Lamb of God.

The feast promises refreshment, as the participant is offered water. Milk provides nourishment; thus the feaster will be fed. There is also great exhilaration and enjoyment—celebration—as wine for all is included.

Who is to come? The exiles in Babylon, yearning for their homeland, found comfort in the promise of security and celebration. Material blessings would follow their return to Israel.

55:2, 3 Because God gives the sustenance of physical and spiritual life freely, why would anyone want to "spend money on what is not bread, and your labor on what does not satisfy"? Some of the Jews in Babylon did not wish to return to Zion because they would have to give up prosperous businesses, established clientele, secure social circles for an uncertain, potentially dangerous future. So they exchanged God's promise for the equivalent of bean soup, as Esau sold his birthright for a bowl of lentil stew. In contrast, those who listen to God, no matter how poor they may be, "will delight in the richest of fare": God's eternal favor, His "everlasting covenant" with His people.

"Give ear and come to me; hear me . . . " indicates that the listener is to focus so that he or she hears only what is being spoken by the One who gives the command. The physical, immediate fulfillment of this prophecy is amplified to include spiritual, eternal benefits with the phrase, "that your soul may live."

God initiates a covenant, an everlasting relationship of *hesed,* the "faithful love promised to David." This is the steadfast love, the *hesed* of God so prominent in the Psalms of David on which the shepherd king relied in the midst of despair. For example, Psalm 13 begins, "How long, O Lord?," as David pleads for help, then resolves in David's acknowledgment: "But I trust in your unfailing [steadfast] love" (vs. 5). This was the covenant to which Isaiah referred, a relationship of certainty and permanance.

Seek the Lord (55:6, 7)

55:6 Much effort has been devoted to the preparation of the banquet of salvation. Now, all is ready. God initiates a grand invitation: Come! What a waste to reject this offer. "How shall we escape if we ignore such a great salvation?" wrote the author of Hebrews (2:3a). We haven't the resources, the ability, the possibility to preside over such a feast; therefore, we should be careful to respond to the Lord's invitation "while he may be found." The language indicates that our coming to God is possible only when He desires to be found. Paul clarifies the concept by quoting from Isaiah 49:8: "As God's fellow workers we urge you not to receive God's grace in vain. For he says, 'In the time of my favor I heard you, and in the day of salvation I helped you.' I tell you, now is the time of God's favor, now is the day of salvation" (II Cor. 6:1, 2).

55:7 The response to the Lord's invitation is, simply, repentance. "Let the wicked forsake his way and the evil man his thoughts. Let him turn to the Lord . . . ." The wicked person is to abandon his old life-style; the evil person is to change the way she thinks. The old will be replaced by the new, for God will have mercy on them. God's steadfast, sure love will embrace them: "He will freely pardon." "But now that you have been set free from sin and have become slaves to God," wrote Paul, "the benefit you reap leads to holiness, and the result is eternal life" (Rom. 6:22).

The Effective Word of God (55:8-11)

55:8, 9 To the exiled Jew in Babylon, God's invitation may have seemed a cruel joke. Though he was allowed to prosper in some respects in Babylon, he was not allowed to return to Israel. The possibility of Israel becoming a nation to which other nations bowed (see 55:5) was incomprehensible. The idea of including everybody (see 55:1—"all who are thirsty") was preposterous, even insulting. But God's thoughts and ways, His purposes and designs, are not our thoughts and ways. God, at this point, emphasizes the contrast between His God-ness and our humaneness, "my" versus "your," then "your" versus "my." This "declares the Lord," again stressing the superiority intrinsic in His deity.

As if His listeners don't seem to understand his point, the Lord explains how He is superior in His purposes and designs. "Look, let's keep it simple," He seems to say. "See the sky? Pretty high isn't it? That's how much higher my ways are than your ways." Recent space exploration, rather than demonstrating that humankind can conquer space, has shown us how vast and formidable are the galaxies. The sinful person, redeemed by God's grace, begins to explore His love and mercy, only to find that her understanding is one small planet among galaxies.

55:10, 11 The natural cycles of Creation illustrate the effectiveness of the Word of God. Rain and snow fall; they soak into the earth, watering seeds planted there. As the plant grows, it uses water in photosynthesis or returns the water to the sky through evaporation. In turn, the plant produces grain, which is harvested and made into bread for the eater. These are normal, usual, consistent events, ordered and controlled by God's power.

"So is my word that goes out from my mouth," says the Lord. This is God's Word, the "God-breathed" Scripture of II Timothy 3:16. As Creation has been divinely ordered, God's Word has been divinely ordered. Its very divinity guarantees its effectiveness. "For the word of God is living and active," notes the author of Hebrews (4:12). "Sharper than any double-edged sword, it penetrates even to dividing soul and spirit, joints and marrow; it judges the thoughts and attitudes of the heart." His Word accomplishes its purpose in the lives of the righteous, forming individuals into the likeness of the Son (see Rom. 8:28, 29). When Jesus preached that the fulfillment of Isaiah 53:1 was occurring in His presence ("Lord, who has believed our message . . . ?") He noted how the Word would judge the wicked: "There is a judge for the one who rejects me and does not accept my words; that very word which I spoke will condemn him at the last day" (Jn. 12:48). God's Word will inevitably effectively complete the job.

For Discussion

1. How have you seen God's faithful, steadfast love shown to you (see vss. 3, 7)? How have you shown His mercy to others?

2. C. S. Lewis speaks of a "sweet longing" that we all seem to experience in this life. How have you experienced this longing in your own life? Will it ever be satisfied?

3. If you were to chart the last two or three years, with one column noting how you planned things and another noting what God actually did, how would they be similar? Different? Do you see God's thoughts and ways affecting your thinking so that your plans originate with God, and thus come to pass?

Window on the Word

One Book in His Pack

When Stanley started across the continent of Africa he had 73 books in three packs, weighing 180 pounds. After he had gone three hundred miles, he was obliged to throw away some of his books, through the fatigue of those carrying his baggage. As he continued on his journey, his library grew less and less, until he had but one book left. You can imagine its name—the Bible. It is said that he read that Book through three times during the journey.

9

The Service God Seeks

Truth to Apply: God wants me to worship Him by helping the poor and oppressed.

Key Verse: Is not this the kind of fasting I have chosen: to loose the chains of injustice and untie the cords of the yoke, to set the oppressed free and break every yoke? (Isa. 58:6)

As Pilgrim continued on his journey to be rid of the burden on his back . . . he was met by Mr. Worldly Wiseman.

Mr. Worldly Wiseman proceeded as follows:

"Hear me—I am older than you—and I'll give you some advice. In yonder village there dwells a gentleman whose name is Legality, a very judicious man—a man of very good name. He has skill to help men off with their burdens. He has, to my knowledge, cured several who were going out of their wits because of them. His house is not a mile from this place, and if he's not at home himself, his son—who's called Civility—will help you. Moreover, if you wish, there are houses standing empty in the village at reasonable rates. The food is cheap and good, and you can send for your wife and family, and all live happily together" (John Bunyan, *Dangerous Journey: The Story of Pilgrim's Progress,* Eerdmans, 1985).

What are the advantages with which Worldly Wiseman tempts Christian? Why is following rules an easier road than making decisions—especially decisions to help others in need? Do you have any examples?

Background/Overview: *Isaiah 58:5-11*

While Assyria, the dominant military power during Isaiah's time, was destroying the Northern Kingdom of Israel, Isaiah was prophesying in the Southern Kingdom, Judah. Ultimately the Assyrian forces reached the walls of Jerusalem, but were defeated by God's supernatural intervention (Isa. 37:36). Isaiah lived in the expanding shadows of the Assyrian empire.

Isaiah condemned evil practices among the Jews, as well as among the surrounding nations. He invited all to repent and reform, with comforting promises of a coming Messiah. But it was an uphill battle. The division of the kingdom following Solomon's reign, brought a succession of inept and evil monarchs to both the north and south.

Like other prophets of the Lord, Isaiah condemned not only outright idolatry, but also the practice of the rituals of religion without regard for the welfare of one's neighbor.

Light on the Text

Outward Conformity (58:5)

Verse 5 of chapter 58 is a response to the first four verses, in which Isaiah depicts the people of Israel doing outward fasting, but without inner repentance. "They ask me for just decisions," the Lord says, "and seem eager for God to come near them" (vs. 2). But their fasting "ends in quarreling and strife . . ." (vs. 4). "You cannot fast as you do today," groans God, "and expect your voice to be heard on high" (vs. 4).

The questions of verse 5, then, already have been answered.

"Is this the kind of fast I have chosen, only a day for a man to humble himself?" he asks. The sound and sense reminds Isaiah's listeners of his earlier messages from the Lord: "Stop bringing meaningless offerings!" (Isa. 1:13a). Pretending to be humble just by "bowing one's head like a reed and . . . lying on sackcloth and ashes" is nothing but a charade. Fasting was not intended to be spiritually fashionable, but intensely personal.

The people of Judah, with their love for Jerusalem and their strong attachment to Temple worship, sacrifices, assemblies, and holy days (see Isa. 1), found simple piety too unstructured. Jesus found the same problem when He discussed salvation with an expert in the Law. "What is written in the Law?" He asked. The Law expert answered, " 'Love the Lord your God with all your heart and with all your soul and with all your strength and with all your mind'; and 'Love your neighbor as yourself.' "

"You have answered correctly," Jesus replied. "Do this and you will live" (Lk. 10:26-28). But that was too unstructured, too difficult for the Law expert, because "he wanted to justify himself." If following the Law meant that one's good deeds were the result of a pure heart, the application was not so clear-cut, or uncomplicated, or simple.

Loosing the Chains (58:6, 7)

58:6 Another question: "Is not this the kind of fasting I have chosen . . . ?" The answer is contained in the question: "to loose the chains of injustice . . . to set the oppressed free . . . ?"

This is a more difficult worship, for it involves working within unjust systems to execute justice; it may involve tearing down unjust systems to create new, just structures. Martin Luther King, Jr., was conscious of the complications involved in attempting to restructure unjust systems to provide social, economic, and political freedom for his oppressed black brothers and sisters: "This dynamic unity, this amazing self-respect, this willingness to suffer, and this refusal to hit back will soon cause the oppressor to become ashamed of his own methods. . . . There is nothing in all the world greater than freedom. It is worth paying for; it is worth losing a job; it is worth going to jail for" (*A Testament of Hope: The Essential Writings of Martin Luther King, Jr.*, Harper & Row, 1986).

58:7 The Lord asks for simple acts of kindness, as well. "Is it not to share your food with the hungry and to provide the poor wanderer with shelter . . . ?" The reminder "not to turn away from your own flesh and blood" (see also Gen. 29:13, 14) possibly denotes humankind generally. To turn away from one's own flesh and blood is to refuse to act humanely toward anyone who is in need, as Jesus so sharply pointed out in the parable of the good Samaritan.

Light, Healing, Righteousness! (58:8-11)

58:8 These verses find their New Testament equivalent in Galatians 6:7, 8: "A man reaps what he sows. The one who sows to please his sinful nature, from that nature will reap destruction; the one who sows to please the Spirit, from the Spirit will reap eternal life." This passage in Isaiah describes in both symbolic and literal language what we can expect if the behavior described in verses six and seven becomes the pattern of our lives. As the light of day breaks open the night, especially in the desert, so "your light will break forth like the dawn." As a plant that sprouts up overnight, "your healing will quickly appear."

Two parallel expressions constitute the second half of verse eight. "Your righteousness" (or "your righteous One") and "the glory of the Lord" form the honor guard and the rear guard. God will saturate His people with His light, His healing, and His righteousness. He will precede and follow His people.

58:9 "Then you will call" refers back to verse two, when superficial worshippers "seek me out" and are not heard. When His people have repented, then "the Lord will answer." The rest of verse nine and the first half of verse ten reiterate verse six. Do you want to know how to please the Lord, how to get Him to listen to your cry for help? Then do these things: Set the oppressed free. Feed the hungry. Clothe the naked. Stop malicious talk.

58:10 "Spend yourselves" summarizes the manner in which one is to serve others. The Revised Standard Version reads, "If you pour yourself out for the hungry . . . ." Much of the value of the gift lies in the attitude and motives of the giver, in the *manner* of giving. When John Perkins, founder of Mendenhall Ministries, went back to Mississippi to work among the poor, he says, "Right away I started to work, cutting wood and picking cotton. . . . I was not a 'have' giving handouts to 'have nots.' I had given up a good job, a big comfortable house, and the freedom and respect I had enjoyed in California to return to the poverty, discomfort, and oppression I had left behind 13 years earlier. . . . To reach my people I was following the same pattern Jesus had used to reach me" (*With Justice For All,* Gospel Light, 1982).

58:11 The abundance of God's blessing is depicted here. In a sun-scorched land, one that always needs more water, less wind, more greenery, less sand, "The Lord will guide you always; he will satisfy your needs." Blessing is added to blessing. Not only will needs be satisfied, but He "will strengthen your frame," invigorating and rejuvenating His people. Survival is enough to ask for, but God's people will be "like a well-watered garden, like a spring whose waters never fail," both unlikely possibilities in the desert. Nonetheless, as the nation of Israel was able to return to her home and flourish in the desert, so have the spiritual people of God flourished wherever God has established His church.

For Discussion

1. What are some religious acts that are often used as substitutes for true religion? Why do people do these things? Why does God find these "sacrifices" unacceptable?

2. If you worship in a more liturgical setting, how can your liturgy become meaningless ritual? What clues for revitalizing your worship can you find in Isaiah 58:6, 7? If you worship in a (so-called) nonliturgical setting, how can the Sunday routine become meaningless ritual? What might you do to revitalize it? What are the benefits of each of these forms of worship?

3. What kind of worship/fast is what God has chosen? What does it mean to "loose the chains of injustice"?

What can you do in your own church and neighborhood to practice this kind of Sabbath? What can you do that will most surely inconvenience you? Should you do it anyway? Will you?

4. What does it mean to "spend yourselves"? What dangers are implicit for those in professional Christian ministry (i.e., missionaries, pastors, those working in Christian organizations)? What dangers are implicit for those who do not "spend themselves" but simply do "good deeds"?

Window on the Word

Speed Up That Day

"I have a dream that one day on the red hills of Georgia, sons of former slaves and sons of former slave-owners will be able to sit down together at the table of brotherhood.

"I have a dream that one day, even the state of Mississippi, a state sweltering with the heat of injustice, sweltering with the heat of oppression, will be transformed into an oasis of freedom and justice. . . .

"I have a dream that one day every valley shall be exalted, every hill and mountain shall be made low, the rough places shall be made plain, and the crooked places shall be made straight and the glory of the Lord will be revealed and all flesh shall see it together.

"This is our hope. . . . So let freedom ring. . . .

"And when we allow freedom to ring, when we let it ring from every village and hamlet, from every state and city, we will be able to speed up that day when all of God's children—black men and white men, Jews and Gentiles, Catholics and Protestants—will be able to join hands and to sing in the words of the old Negro spiritual, 'Free at last, free at last; thank God Almighty, we are free at last.' "

(*A Testament of Hope: The Essential Writings of Martin Luther King, Jr.*, Harper & Row, 1986)

10

A New Day for God's People

Truth to Apply: God wants me to promote His peace and to display Christ's righteousness.

Key Verse: They will be called the Holy People, the Redeemed of the Lord (Isa. 62:12a).

Nearly 23 million United States households were touched by crime in 1984. Five percent of those households had a member victimized by violent crime. The National Crime Survey says that a relative of the victim was identified as the offender in 7 percent of all violent victimizations measured during 1973-81. This represents 4.1 million violent victimizations by relatives during this nine-year period. (*World Almanac*, 1986)

World population has just passed the 5 billion mark. By 2000, more than half of those people will live in cities, with Mexico City spilling over with 27.6 million people and New York (sixth on the list) with 19.5 million.

White males, the population group with the most advanced educations, greatest number of opportunities, highest income levels, also had the highest suicide rate in 1981 in the U S.

How do you feel when you read these statistics? Do you think you can do anything to change a world like this? Is there hope?

Background/Overview: *Isaiah 2:2-4; 62:1-3*

Isaiah's world was not so different from ours. His ministry began in the year King Uzziah died and continued through the reigns of Jotham, Ahaz, and Hezekiah, kings of Judah. A contemporary of the prophets Amos, Hosea, and Micah, he was a historian (II Chron. 26:22), a poet, and a prophet. With accuracy, beauty, and authority, Isaiah details God's judgment on rebels and His salvation from Christ.

His prophecy begins (Chapter 1) with a description of rebellion, domestic and international violence, a desolate country without hope. Corruption permeated Israel, from king down to slave. Even the "religious" people who went to the Temple every Sabbath day were leading dissolute lives. Isaiah's prophecy is not just doom and destruction, however, but a cry for action: "Stop doing wrong, learn to do right! Seek justice, encourage the oppressed" (Isa. 1:16b, 17a). Isaiah calls God's people to change. What's more, he offers the Messiah as the definition, the incarnation, of God's peace, justice, and righteousness. There *is* hope!

Light on the Text

Marching to Zion (2:2-4)

2:2 Isaiah's call to worship on "the mountain of the Lord's temple" parallels Micah 4:1-3. In each case, the prophecy is followed by a resolution to follow the Lord (Isa. 2:5; Mic. 4:5).

When will this river of people seek the Lord? "In the last days," says Isaiah, the days initiated by the arrival of the Messiah and completed by His Second Coming, say some scholars. Other scholars say the last days will be initiated by the Second Coming of Christ. During Isaiah's time, the Temple was located on top of a small hill called Zion. It was considered to be God's specific dwelling place. Pagan gods also had their mountains: Olympus, Capitol, Albordash, Merie, Zaphon and so on. Here the prophet proclaims that someday Mount Zion will be exalted above all others; that is, God will be exalted above all the so-called gods. The word "established" connotes durability, permanence. The psalmist uses this word to speak of God's rule over the earth: "The world is firmly established; it cannot be moved. Your throne was established long ago; you are from all eternity" (Ps. 93:1b, 2).

In the Hebrew poetic tradition, the prophet repeats this thought in a parallel clause: "it will be raised above the hills." Because sacrifices were offered on hilltops to pagan deities, the thought is reinforced. God will reign supreme.

The people in the vision, representing all nations, are compared to rivers flowing up the sides of Zion. This image is reflected in Jeremiah 51:44, where the prophet pronounces that "the nations will no longer stream to [Sheshach]" (a pagan nation). Instead of streaming to foreign gods, representatives of all nations will seek the Lord. The Lord was considered by outsiders a local, Israelite deity. Worship of Him was, for the most part, confined to Israel. In Isaiah's prophecy of the last days, however, worship of the Lord will extend to the ends of the earth—"all nations."

2:3 People from all nations are converging on Zion because they know that there they will learn from the true God, the "God of Jacob," whom Israel and her ancestors have revered. The worshipers reveal their genuine desire to please God by encouraging others to accompany them ("Come, let us go up to the mountain of the Lord") and by resolving to "walk in his paths." Other nations will look to Zion, says Isaiah, "to the brightness of your dawn. . . . your heart will throb and swell with joy" (Isa. 60:3, 5). The Spirit of the Sovereign Lord bestows "the oil of gladness instead of mourning, and a garment of praise instead of a spirit of despair" (Isa. 61:3). This eager desire to serve God is a remarkable contrast to the attitude pagans had toward serving their gods. Foreign gods were not benevolent teachers; the Lord, however, teaches with compassion and care.

The pilgrims are coming to Zion because there they can find the truth they seek: "The law will go out from Zion, the word of the Lord from Jerusalem." The emphasis here is on the phrases "from Zion" and "from Jerusalem." This is a triumphant proclamation that "salvation is from the Jews" (Jn. 4:22). The holiness of Sinai, where God first appeared to His people Israel, was transplanted to Zion. Later, the holiness that was epitomized by Zion would be incarnated in Jesus Christ, "the source of eternal salvation for all who obey him" (Heb. 5:10).

2:4 The spiritual responsiveness of the people who go to the mountain of the Lord has entirely reshaped their world. The Lord will arbitrate their conflicts, with the inevitable result that humanity's great curse—war—will cease. Instead, "they will beat their swords into plowshares and their spears into pruning hooks."

Weapons of death will be transformed into tools for growth. The rhythm of these verses reflects the beauty of the peace for which we long: "Nation will not take up sword against nation, nor will they train for war anymore." Weapons of war will not be destroyed, but transformed into instruments of peace, tools to make the world fair and fruitful. The absence of war is not enough; God's people must learn peace, must "seek peace and pursue it" (Ps. 34:14).

O Zion Haste (62:1-3)

62:1 This triumphant poem (vss. 1-3) proclaims the urgency of persevering until the day of God's salvation. Isaiah will not rest until God brings salvation to Israel. He perseveres "for Zion's sake . . . for Jerusalem's sake"; he is energized by the certainty of final victory ("The nations will see your righteousness . . . you will be called by a new name" [vs. 2]). The Lord will not rest until He has brought salvation to Israel. God will continue to speak and act on Zion's behalf. He reinforces His tenacity in verse 6: "I have posted watchmen on your walls, O Jerusalem; they will never be silent day or night." Thus it is the Lord who continues to work, setting an example for all who serve Him. God refuses to stop working until His salvation is accomplished.

At this point, Zion is unnoticed by the rest of the world. Yet, says the prophet, her righteousness will shine "out like the dawn." This is no slow sunrise over a sleepy village, but a light that bursts through the night. Earlier Isaiah says, "your light will break forth like the dawn" (58:8). Zion's righteousness will startle the world with its brilliance, "like a blazing torch" in the middle of a dark night.

62:2 The nations will not merely see this righteousness; they will pay attention to it. All kings, not just a few, will acknowledge the glory which is greater than their own. Because Zion will have a new nature, God will mark His people with a name designating their holy character. This name will embody the essence of the people. God called Abram "Abraham" when He chose him to father the new nation of Israel; later He named Jacob "Israel." God, in pledging Himself to Zion, would call her Hephzibah ("my delight is in her") and Beulah ("married"), instead of Deserted and Desolate (vs. 4).

62:3 The word pictures in verse 3 convey the grandeur of the work of the Lord's hand. "You will be a crown of splendor," He says, "a royal diadem in the hand of your God." Dressed as royalty—a high priest or a king—Zion will rule with brilliance and authority. She will not govern independently, however, but in the Lord's hand. Her place in the Lord's hand also portrays her relationship to God. As in Proverbs 12:4a, where "a wife of noble character is her husband's crown," so is Zion, the recipient of God's love and affection.

The Method Is Important!

When we as Christians seek to promote righteousness and peace, we need to be wary of the illusion that we can best do so by pointing out the faults of others. Criticism triggers a self-protective instinct in the person criticized. Any judgment of another's behavior or attitudes is, on the natural, instinctive level, seen as an attack that is met with the natural responses of fight or flight. We may feel that our motives are pure, but the end result is that we often reap resentment and hostility.

Paul Tournier points out: "The most tragic consequence of our criticism of a man is to block his way to [humility] and grace, precisely to drive him into the mechanisms of self-justification and into his faults instead of freeing him from them. For him, our voice drowns the voice of God."

This is not to say that there is no place for speaking the truth in love. But avoid a judgmental self-righteousness. Jesus' advice should guide us: "First take the plank out of your own eye, and then you will see clearly to remove the speck from your brother's eye" (Mt. 7:5).

For Discussion

1. If Mount Zion was God's "specific dwelling place" in Isaiah's day, where does He dwell today? What has happened since Isaiah to cause this change? (See Heb. 9 for further discussion.)

2. How might God's people encourage others to join them? What further reasons might His Church offer for seeking the Lord ("He will teach us his ways, so that we may walk in his paths" [2:3])?

3. How do you think you should view nuclear disarmament—or buildup—in light of these Scriptures? In what ways can God's Church beat swords into plowshares? Is this activity intended to be a continuing one, or should it happen all at once (not until the Second Coming, for instance), or gradually, with culmination at a given point in history? Discuss.

4. What nation will be noticed by the rest of the world for her righteousness? Is this a political nation—Israel, America, Canada, England—or a spiritual nation, God's Church? What responsibility does this nation have? In what ways should she display her righteousness?

5. Consider your relationship with God. Are you a "crown of splendor" in His hand, providing leadership? What are some examples of how you do this? Are you "a

wife of noble character," eager to tell others that you are the object of God's love and affection? How have you done this?

Window on the Word

Turning Evil into Good

One of the Greek philosophers wrote: "And this is the greatest stroke of art, to turn an evil into a good."

Christians from South Africa converted a shell found on the battlefields into a bell for a church. Former derelicts from Los Angeles' skid row return to the streets to minister to former cronies. Ex-con Charles Colson formed Prison Fellowship to minister to the needs of convicts and their families. Jerry Onufrock, a boy who hated Sunday School, is now a fourth-grade Sunday School teacher who is determined to make his class inspirational.

These Christians are transforming hurtful experiences into beneficial ones. Have you joined them in this vital mission?

11

Good News for The Poor

Truth to Apply: God's salvation means I have good news of healing, freedom, and comfort for those in need.

Key Verse: "The Spirit of the Sovereign Lord is on me, because the Lord has anointed me to preach good news to the poor" (Isa. 61:1).

The poor are everywhere, in cities and rural areas, hidden in wealthy neighborhoods and lying out on the streets. To be poor is to be powerless; even in court systems that are relatively ethical, money often speaks louder than truth. The brokenhearted are everywhere. The most publicized suicides are among well-to-do, suburban young people—kids who have everything, but who are desolate of heart. The injustices of the apartheid system leave entire communities of women and children with broken hearts, separated from their menfolk by zoning ordinances. The captive are everywhere. The wealthy, with freedom to enjoy unrestrained leisure, are the group most chained to cocaine use. Prisons are in havoc as their populations multiply before adequate facilities can be built to accommodate new convicts.

What can we do about the poor, the brokenhearted and the captive? Are they a "problem" too big to solve? Why?

Background/Overview: *Isaiah 61*

For all of Isaiah's influence, we know very little about him. We do know that he married a prophetess and had at least two sons (Isa. 7:3; 8:3). Since his major work as an historian, as far as we know, was to record the events of Uzziah's reign, he may have been a court chronicler as well as a prophet. That would explain not only his ease of access to the king and the royal court, but also his wide knowledge of foreign affairs and his skill as a writer.

His name is a compound of two words that mean "the Lord saves," or more explicitly, "the Lord is the source of salvation." Given the significance placed on an individual's name in Bible times, it is fascinating to note that "save" and "salvation" are among his favorite words. In many ways, Isaiah was a living embodiment of the truth that salvation is to be found in the Lord.

In Isaiah 61, the prophet explains who has sent him, what he is to do, where his work is to be done, why he must preach and when all this will happen. So even though we don't know much about Isaiah's external life, we may discover his inner life—his sensitivity to justice and righteousness, his perseverence and persistence, his compassion and tenderness toward the downtrodden.

Light on the Text

The Anointed One (61:1-3)

61:1 Who is the person speaking here? Certainly Isaiah was referring to himself, declaring himself the prophet of the Lord whose words were authoritative and applicable in his context. As has been noted, the prophet's character and calling are reflected in his words.

However, the Trinitarian nature of this verse cannot be ignored. When Jesus read the Scriptures in His hometown synagogue one Sabbath day, "he found the place where it is written: 'The Spirit of the Lord is on me, because he has anointed me . . .' Then he rolled up the scroll, gave it back to the attendant and sat down. . . . and he began by saying to them, 'Today this scripture is fulfilled in your hearing' " (Luke 4:16-21). The Holy Spirit of the Lord Yahweh is the Spirit of the all-powerful God, who anointed Jesus to preach the Good News (see also Mt. 3:13-17).

The Hebrew word translated "preach good news" is picturesque. The same verb is found in Jeremiah 20:15, where it refers to the good news of the birth of a son, which makes the father "very glad."

With God's salvation comes a new society. As individuals in corrupt societies are restored, their influence adds another girder to the structure of that new society. Every humane landlord, every fair employer, every medical professional volunteering in a refugee camp is part of God's (salty, Mt. 5:13) Good News to the poor. And every individual who confesses herself poor before God finds hope and restoration in the Good News. "Come to me, all you who are weary and burdened, and I will give you rest," Jesus said, ". . . and you will find rest for your souls" (Mt. 11:28, 29).

The speaker's purpose was also to "bind up the brokenhearted," to restore the broken of heart. Whether weighed down by sin or burdened by life's losses, the good news heals. As with exiled Israel, today's refugees may despair as they think of the homelands to which they may never return. But there is healing and hope in the good news—healing from painful memories and hope for a better city, a better land (see Heb. 11:8-16).

The captivity in which the true Israel of God lay was far deeper than their exile, however. The people were captive to sin. As Luke 4:18 has it, "recovery of sight for the blind" is promised. This is illumined by Paul's explanation that "The god of this age has blinded the minds of unbelievers, so that they cannot see the light of the gospel of the glory of Christ" (II Cor. 4:4).

61:2 Isaiah seems to be referring to the Year of Jubilee. This year, outlined in Leviticus 25, was intended to be a year of liberation and celebration. Isaiah 61:1 summarizes its primary aspects. When Jesus read in the synagogue (Lk. 4:16-21), he stopped short of ". . . the day of vengeance." The Year of Jubilee was initiated by Jesus' ministry, but God's full judgment would come only with Christ's Second Coming. The purpose of Isaiah's proclamation is to "comfort all who mourn."

61:3 The prophet reinforces what he has already said by portraying the difference between a mourning, desolate Zion and the restored people of God. God's gifts are abundant—a "crown of beauty," "the oil of gladness," "a garment of praise." These metaphors display the wealth of the broken spirit renewed by God's Spirit. God's people will be called "oaks of righteousness." The psalmist often portrayed the wicked as "grass," which has a short life span, and bears no fruit, while the righteous are called "oaks" or "cedars of Lebanon," whose roots grow deep and who bear fruit (see Ps. 2:7,12-14).

The Conditions of the Messiah's Kingdom (61:4-7)

The thrust of verses 4-7 is the vindication and restoration of God's people. In Isaiah's context, a rebuilt Jerusalem is in store for a people who will return to their homeland. Foreigners will one day serve the people of Israel who will enjoy their full inheritance as priests and ministers of God. Gentiles will happily bless those in Zion with their wealth.

According to premillennialists, all the promises to Abraham and David will be literally fulfilled, if not before, then during the reign of Jesus Christ on earth. At His Second Coming, Christ will assume the throne of David and actually reign over the earth as king for 1000 years. The events spoken of here will occur during that time (according to a premillennial understanding).

According to amillennialists, the verses refer to the Christian church, the "new Israel," which will include not just ethnic Jews, but Gentiles. The flavor of verse 5 is not that Jews will rule over Gentiles, but that in the Messianic Kingdom all will work together. Those who were once aliens and foreigners because of their alienation from the God of Israel will become God's people, working together to maintain the Church of God, His Kingdom on earth. The Church will thrive on the goods of those who are converted. References to Canaan, the Promised Land, are a powerful figure of speech for the promised blessings of the Messiah.

Whichever of these two views is held, the practical implications are identical in one area: hope for the future. Because of the work of Christ on the cross, both Jew and Gentile can look forward to reigning with him. That is the message of the Gospel Jesus came to proclaim. ". . . And everlasting joy will be theirs."

Good News for the Lonely, Too

Sociologists tell us that the human being is a social creature. That means simply that persons need other persons. God, in Genesis, confirmed that by creating Eve: "It is not good that the man should be alone."

And it's true that in relationships we find the best and the worst of the human. The full range of human potential is displayed: love and hate, blessing and cursing, sacrifice and selfishness.

A lonely person is diminished and unfulfilled. One prisoner in solitary confinement, years afterward, told of gazing into a bit of smoothed foil just to catch a glimpse of a human face, even if it was only his own.

Though we may take them for granted, the relationships that frame and support our way are crucial to our own humanness. And relationships take place primarily in the context of communication—of speech, gestures, laughter, words. We especially need words. We thrive on the give-and-take that makes us known to others as well as to ourselves. Without that we only limp along, and our souls are cramped.

Dialogue, not just conversation, is a high art, requiring the best we have to offer in exchange for the priceless gift of friendship. We should practice it prayerfully.

For Discussion

1. Who are the afflicted or lonely in your church and community? Are there members of your church body who might be counted among the poor, the brokenhearted, the captive? Are their needs physical? spiritual? What is the good word that you can take to them?

2. What might you do to participate in the Year of Jubilee? The celebration described in Leviticus 25 describes a physical, literal release of debtors, slaves, property. Are there acts you can perform as a businessperson, household manager or friend that would express the substance of Jubilee?

3. Think of a public figure who has been recently criminally indicted. How long do you think you will remember his name? Now think of someone you know who has done a good deed. How long will you remember that person's name and her deed?

4. Why was the hope that the prophet Isaiah brought to Israel and Judah so important to them? Why is hope for the future important to you?

Window on the Word

The Good News in a Blanket

In Philadelphia, Pennsylvania, a boy named Trevor indifferently watched the six o'clock news. Then something caught his attention. There was a man sleeping on the sidewalk in Philadelphia, a "street person," the reporter called him. He ran to the den where his parents were watching television. "Do people really live like that?" he asked. "Yes," was the reply. "Then can I take them one of my blankets, Dad? And a pillow?" The boy was insistent; his parents relented, ready more to teach him a lesson on the ugly side of life than to assist him. What began with a pillow and a blanket has grown into a national campaign of caring, with groups in San Diego, California; Oklahoma City, Oklahoma; and New Delhi, India calling themselves chapters of Trevor's Campaign. "Two thousand years ago," his parents say, "a single act of love tipped the balance. We are here to keep that love going. All of us, young and old, can find someone to reach out to in kindness."

(Adapted from *Family Life Today,* February, 1985)

12

Preparing for God's Coming

Truth to Apply: Being called to prepare the way of the Lord, I must analyze the effects of a commercial environment on my celebration of Christ's birth.

Key Verse: A voice of one calling: "In the desert prepare the way for the Lord; make straight in the wilderness a highway for our God" (Isa. 40:3).

The simplicity of Christ's birth has evaded us as we seek to outdo one another with our Christmas gift buying. In 1962, an author for Eternity magazine advocated keeping Santa Claus totally out of the church. He feared that, if we tell children that Santa is a myth, they might apply the same train of thought to Christ and consider him a myth as well. "Ridiculous, isn't it," the author says, "when Christians are decrying the secularization of schools and community life that they often delight in secularizing the church."

But this is our celebration. We Christians, of all people, ought to prepare with joy for the coming of Christ, as remembered in the First Advent and as anticipated in the Second Advent. Have you stopped having birthday parties because some of your friends use them as an excuse for overeating and overdrinking? Of course not! Instead, you show your friends how to celebrate with moderation, remembering whose party it is. In the same way, we need to examine our Christmas traditions and determine if they, indeed, prepare the way for Christ (with love and joy and peace) or if they assist the creeping desert of commercialism (with anxiety and frustration and excess). How might we prepare to celebrate Christ's birth with moderation and simplicity? What might we do to help us think more about Christ's Second Coming?

Background/Overview: *Isaiah 40:3—11*

Israel, condemned for her sin, punished for her negligence, is to be restored. " 'Comfort, comfort my people,' says your God." These opening words declare the shift in themes. The first part of the Book of Isaiah emphasized judgment; salvation and comfort dominate the second part. The judgment of Chapters 1-39 was the purifying force that led to the forgiveness and pardon of sins in Chapters 40-66. "Ultimately," writes John A. Martin in *The Bible Knowledge Commentary: Old Testament* (Victor Books, 1985), "redemption for Israel must come from the 'ideal Servant,' the Messiah, who will accomplish what the servant-nation cannot do." But these chapters go beyond redemption from sin to speak of a change in the cosmos, of the Lord's restoration of His created order, says Martin. While Chapters 1—39 speak of judgment for sin, Chapters 40—66 discuss not only salvation, but the resulting change in people and the world system. Blessing from God is not just a single act; the act of salvation is followed by a whole life of blessing.

Light on the Text

Get Ready for the Glory of the Lord (40:3-5)

40:3, 4 A voice is calling out a command: "In the desert prepare the way for the Lord." This voice is not that of God, for he is referred to in the last part of the verse as "our God." Rather, the voice is that of Isaiah, as prophets were "voices from God." To whom was he referring? In his context, he was certainly telling the Israelites individually to prepare their spiritual lives for the appearing of the Lord and of His glory. Some commentators look to the exiles in Babylon and to their return from their long captivity back to their homeland. While this was a partial fulfillment of the verse, the primary application for us is to John the Baptist. Each of the Gospel writers recited verse 3 in reference to John the Baptist (see Mt. 3:1-4; Mk. 1:1-4; Lk. 1:76-78). In

John 1:23, John the Baptist himself quotes the verse as applying to him.

So it was that John the Baptist, a prophet who lived in the desert, prepared the way for the coming of the Messiah. But there is more to this desert scene. "Prepare the way" suggests turning aside obstacles that may be in the way, ordering and arranging, as a bulldozer clears the path of trees and levels the land, and the highway department erects fences and sound barriers. Then the crew arrives to construct a highway that can be easily traveled. The construction of the Pennsylvania Turnpike was an engineering marvel; nowhere does the road grade exceed 3 degrees. Every valley was raised up; every mountain and hill made low; the rough ground became level, and the rugged places a plain. What the traveler notices, however, is how easily it is traversed. That was to be the marvel of preparation for the Lord's coming—not just a highway, but a level one, not just confession of and forgiveness for sins, but "fruit in keeping with repentance" as well (Mt. 3:8).

40:5 "And the glory of the Lord will be revealed." Have we seen His glory? "We have seen his glory," testifies the apostle John, "the glory of the one and only Son, who came from the Father, full of grace and truth." His glory is displayed in the continuing salvation of His people, the riches of His grace, the extent of His love. But there is more glory to be revealed, and that not in an isolated cattle stall. "All mankind together will see it." Thus we look forward to the Second Advent, when the glory of the Lord will be fully unveiled, when His splendor will be evident everywhere. The glory that is present in the lives of His people will be evident to all.

All these things will occur because, quite simply, "the mouth of the Lord has spoken." The word of the Lord is sure; it cannot be broken.

He Is the God of Always (40:6-8)

"A voice says, 'Cry out.' " But what is the prophet to cry? Cry this: that people are fragile as grass. Even in their glory, they are as weak as wildflowers. When the breath of the Lord blows on the grass, it withers. When the breath of the Lord blows on the flowers, they fall. Before the rainy season in Palestine, the Sirocco wind blows in from the desert regions of Arabia. It blows for several days without intermission, filling the air with fine dust. It sucks the moisture from the air, from the soil, and from the vegetation. That is what people are like when the breath of the Lord blows on them. Now, this is what God is like: His word stands forever. He is permanent. His glory does not rise and fall, it endures.

"The word of our God" refers to "every word that comes from the mouth of God" (Deut. 8:3; Mt. 4:4). While Isaiah's hearers would see the immediate connection with the promise in verse 2 ("Speak tenderly to Jerusalem . . . that her hard service has been completed . . .), Peter applied this verse to the Gospel itself: " ' . . . the word of the Lord stands forever.' And this is the word that was preached to you" (1 Pet. 1:25).

Even more vivid, however, is the contrast between the transitory nature of human beings and the absolute permanence of God's Word. The Word, in its dual revelation as Christ and the Scriptures, lasts forever.

Announce the Good News! (40:9-11)

The announcement of God's presence among His people is to be shouted from a high mountain, loudly, boldly. God's people everywhere, then, are to declare the good news with courage. God's church is not to keep the message of His salvation to herself, but to present it to the world. She is not to pose as a seeker after truth, but to conduct herself as the possesser of truth, with a generous supply at hand. "She must be vigorously and militantly evangelistic," writes Edward J. Young (*The Book of Isaiah, 3,* NICOT, Eerdmans, 1972). "Hesitation, timorousness and trembling are out of place. There is no need to fear as though the Word of God would not be fulfilled, or as though the message would prove to be untrue and embarrassment would result." Verses 10 and 11 portray two diverse characteristics of God: His powerful strength and His tender touch. The work to be done requires a God of strength, whether it be deliverance of Israel from exile in Babylon or deliverance of people from sin. He comes—even now he comes—to rule with His strong arm, bringing under His power everything that stands in His way. "For when you did awesome things that we did not expect, you came down," writes the prophet (64:3), "and the mountains trembled before you." The Israel of Isaiah's day could stand with confidence behind the God who was their advocate; today we can be confident of the God who still acts on behalf of His people.

But this God who roars through a valley like a tornado, terrorizing the trees and bending the wheat to the earth (see Psa. 77:16-20), also walks among His sheep. He does the complete work of shepherding—feeding, watering, sheltering. Again, His arms act, this time to gather the lambs and carry them close to His heart. What a comfort to the lamb, to feel the warmth of the shepherd, to hear the heartbeat that reminds him of his mother's own heartbeat. Tenderly, gently, God cares for His people, not from a big house on a hill, but from among them, where he knows them intimately, and they know him. This is how Jerusalem is comforted: first, "she has received from the Lord's hand double for all her sins" (40:2); now, "he tends his flock like a shepherd" (v.11).

For Discussion

1. What do verses 3-5 promise? How does the permanence of the Lord's Word affect those promises? How might these verses help you when you doubt whether you can see God's glory in your own life, in the lives of other believers, even in your living environment?

2. When Jesus arose from the dead, His disciples "proceeded to announce these joyful tidings with tireless zeal and boundless enthusiasm," says Michael Green in *Evangelism in the Early Church* (Eerdmans, 1982). How does this compare with how the messenger in verse 9 is to act? How does this compare with how you, as a messenger of the Gospel, declare the Good News?

3. What are the images portrayed in verses 10 and 11? Who do these images apply to? How does the image of strength affect you? the image of a shepherd? When do

you need to see yourself as one coming under the arm of power and rule? When do you need to see yourself as a lamb in the arms of a shepherd?

Window on the Word

The Wisest Gift

There were two possessions of the James Dillingham Youngs in which they both took a mighty pride. One was Jim's gold watch that had been his father's and his grandfather's. The other was Della's hair. Had the Queen of Sheba lived in the flat across the airshaft, Della would have let her hair hang out the window some day to dry just to depreciate Her Majesty's jewels and gifts. Had King Solomon been the janitor, with all his treasures piled up in the basement, Jim would have pulled out his watch every time he passed, just to see him pluck at his beard from envy.

Unable to bear Christmas without giving one another gifts, the two sacrifice their beloved possessions. Della sells her long hair so that she can buy a chain for Jim's watch . . . and Jim sells his watch so that he can buy Della combs for her hair.

"The magi, as you know, were wise men—wonderfully wise men—who brought gifts to the Babe in the manger. They invented the art of giving Christmas presents. Being wise, their gifts were no doubt wise ones, possibly bearing the privilege of exchange in case of duplication. And here I have lamely related to you the uneventful chronicle of two foolish children in a flat who most unwisely sacrificed for each other the greatest treasures of their house. But in a last word to the wise of these days let it be said that of all who give gifts these two were the wisest. Of all who give and receive gifts, such as they are wisest. Everywhere they are wisest. They are the magi."

("The Gift of the Magi," *The Complete Works of O. Henry*, Doubleday, 1953)

Leader Helps and Lesson Plan

General Guidelines for Group Study

*Open and close each session with prayer.

*Since the lesson texts are not printed in the book, group members should have their Bibles with them for each study session.

*As the leader, prepare yourself for each session through personal study (during the week) of the Bible text and lesson. On notepaper, jot down any points of interest or concern as you study. Jot down your thoughts about how God is speaking to you through the text, and how He might want to speak to the entire group. Look up cross-reference passages (as they are referred to in the lessons), and try to find answers to questions that come to your mind. Also, recall stories from your own life experience that could be shared with the group to illustrate points in the lesson.

*Try to get participation from everyone. Get to know the more quiet members through informal conversation before and after the sessions. Then, during the study, watch for nonverbal signs (a change in expression or posture) that they would like to respond. Call on them. Say: "What are your thoughts on this, Sue?"

*Don't be afraid of silence. Adults need their own space. Often a long period of silence after a question means the group has been challenged to do some real thinking—hard work that can't be rushed!

*Acknowledge each contribution. No question is a dumb question. Every comment, no matter how "wrong," comes from a worthy person, who needs to be affirmed as valuable to the group. Find ways of tactfully accepting the speaker while guiding the discussion back on track: "Thank you for that comment, John; now what do some of the others think?" or, "I see your point, but are you aware of . . . ?"

When redirecting the discussion, however, be sensitive to the fact that sometimes the topic of the moment *should be* the "sidetrack" because it hits a felt need of the participants.

*Encourage *well-rounded* Christian growth. Christians are called to grow in knowledge of the Word, but they are also challenged to grow in love and wisdom. This means that they must constantly develop in their ability to wisely apply the Bible knowledge to their experience.

Lesson Plan

The following four-step lesson plan can be used effectively for each chapter, varying the different suggested approaches from lesson to lesson.

STEP 1: *Focus on Life Need*

The opening section of each lesson is an anecdote, quote, or other device designed to stimulate sharing on how the topic relates to practical daily living. There are many ways to do this. For example, you might list on the chalkboard the group's answers to: "How have you found this theme relevant to your daily life?" "What are your past successes, or failures, in this area?" "What is your present level of struggle or victory with this?" "Share a story from your own experience relating to this topic."

Sharing questions are designed to be open-ended and allow people to talk about themselves. The questions allow for sharing about past experiences, feelings, hopes and dreams, fears and anxieties, faith, daily life, likes and dislikes, sorrows and joys. Self-disclosure results in group members' coming to know each other at a more intimate level. This kind of personal sharing is necessary to experience deep affirmation and love.

However you do it, the point is to get group members to share *where they are now* in relation to the Biblical topic. As you seek to get the group involved, remember the following characteristics of good sharing questions:[1]

1. Good sharing questions encourage risk without forcing participants to go beyond their willingness to respond.

2. Good sharing questions begin with low risk and build toward higher risk. (It is often good, for instance, to ask a history question to start, then build to present situations in people's lives.)

3. Sharing questions should not require people to confess their sins or to share only negative things about themselves.

4. Questions should be able to be answered by every member of the group.

5. The questions should help the group members to know one another better and learn to love and understand each other more.

6. The questions should allow for enough diversity in response so each member does not wind up saying the same thing.

7. They should ask for sharing of self, not for sharing of opinions.

STEP 2: *Focus on Bible Learning*

Use the "Light on the Text" section for this part of the lesson plan. Again, there are a number of ways to get group members involved, but the emphasis here is more on learning Bible content than on applying it. Below are some suggestions on how to proceed. The methods could be varied from week to week.

*Lecture on important points in the Bible passage (from your personal study notes).

*Assign specific verses in the Bible passage to individuals. Allow five or ten minutes for them to jot down 1) questions, 2) comments, 3) points of concern raised by the text. Then have them share in turn what they have written down.

*Pick important or controversial verses from the passage. In advance, do a personal study to find differences of interpretation among commentators. List and explain these "options" on a blackboard and invite comments concerning the relative merits of each view. Summarize and explain your own view, and challenge other group members to further study.

*Have class members do their own outline of the Bible passage. This is done by giving an original title to each section, chapter, and paragraph, placing each under its appropriate heading according to subject matter. Share the outlines and discuss.

*Make up your own sermons from the Bible passage. Each sermon could include: Title, Theme Sentence, Outline, Illustration, Application, Benediction. Share and discuss.

*View works of art based on the text. Discuss.

*Individually, or as a group, paraphrase the Bible passage in your own words. Share and discuss.

*Have a period of silent meditation upon the Bible passage. Later, share insights.

STEP 3: *Focus on Bible Application*

Most adults prefer group discussion above any other learning method. Use the "For Discussion" section for each lesson to guide a good discussion on the lesson topic and how it relates to felt needs.

Students can benefit from discussion in a number of important ways:[2]

1. Discussion stimulates interest and thinking, and helps students develop the skills of observation, analysis, and hope.
2. Discussion helps students clarify and review what they have learned.
3. Discussion allows students to hear opinions that are more mature and perhaps more Christlike than their own.
4. Discussion stimulates creativity and aids students in applying what they have learned.
5. When students verbalize what they believe and are forced to explain or defend what they say, their convictions are strengthened and their ability to share what they believe with others is increased.

There are many different ways to structure a discussion. All have group interaction as their goal. All provide an opportunity to share in the learning process.

But using different structures can add surprise to a discussion. It can mix people in unique ways. It can allow new people to talk.

Total Class Discussion

In some small classes, all students are able to participate in one effective discussion. This can build a sense of class unity, and it allows everyone to hear the wisdom of peers. But in most groups, total class discussion by itself is unsatisfactory because there is usually time for only a few to contribute.

Buzz Groups

Small groups of three to ten people are assigned any topic for discussion. They quickly select a chairperson and a secretary. The chairperson is responsible for keeping the discussion on track, and the secretary records the group's ideas, reporting the relevant ones to the total class.

Brainstorming

Students, usually in small groups, are presented with a problem and asked to come up with as many different solutions as possible. Participants should withhold judgment until all suggestions (no matter how creative!) have been offered. After a short break, the group should pick the best contribution from those suggested and refine it. Each brainstorming group will present its solution in a total class discussion.

Forum Discussion

Forum discussion is especially valuable when the subject is difficult and the students would not be able to participate in a meaningful discussion without quite a bit of background. People with special training or experience have insights which would not ordinarily be available to the students. Each forum member should prepare a three- to five-minute speech and be given uninterrupted time in which to present it. Then students should be encouraged to interact with the speakers, either directly or through a forum moderator.

Debate

As students prepare before class for their parts in a debate, they should remember that it is the affirmative side's repsonsibility to prove that the resolve is correct. The negative has to prove that it isn't. Of course, the negative may also want to present an alternative proposal.

There are many ways to structure a debate, but the following pattern is quite effective.

1. First affirmative speech
2. First negative speech
3. Second affirmative speech
4. Second negative speech

(brief break while each side plans its rebuttal)

5. First negative rebuttal
6. First affirmative rebuttal
7. Second negative rebuttal
8. Second affirmative rebuttal.

Floating Panel

Sometimes you have a topic to which almost everyone in the room would have something to contribute, for example: marriage, love, work, getting along with people. For a change of pace, have a floating panel: four or five people, whose names are chosen at random, will become "experts" for several minutes. These people sit in chairs in the front of the room while you and other class members ask them questions. The questions should be experience related. When the panel has been in front for several minutes, enough time for each person to make several comments, draw other names and replace the original members.

Interview As Homework

Ask students to interview someone during the week and present what they learned in the form of short reports the following Sunday.

Interview in Class

Occasionally it is profitable to schedule an in-class interview, perhaps with a visiting missionary or with someone who has unique insights to share with the group. One person can take charge of the entire interview, structuring and asking questions. But whenever possible the entire class should take part. Each student should write a question to ask the guest.

In-Group Interview

Divide the class into groups of three, called triads. Supply all groups with the same question or discussion topic. A in the group interviews B while C listens. Then B interviews C while A listens. Finally C interviews A while B listens. Each interview should take from one to three minutes. When the triads return to the class, each person reports on what was heard rather than said.

Following every class period in which you use discussion, ask yourself these questions to help determine the success of your discussion time:

1. In what ways did this discussion contribute to the group's understanding of today's lesson?
2. If each person was not involved, what can I do next week to correct the situation?
3. In what ways did content play a role in the discussion? (I.e., people were not simply sharing off-the-top-of-their-head opinions.)
4. What follow-up, if any, should be made on the discussion? (For example, if participants showed a lack of knowledge, or misunderstanding in some area of Scripture, you may want to cover this subject soon during the class hour. Or, if they discussed decisions they were making or projects they felt the class should be involved in, follow-up outside the class hour may be necessary.)

STEP 4: *Focus on Life Response*

This step tries to incorporate a bridge from the Bible lesson to actual daily living. It should be a *specific* suggestion as to "how we are going to *do* something about this," either individually, or as a group. Though this is a goal to aim for, it is unlikely that everyone will respond to every lesson. But it is good to have a suggested life response ready for that one or two in the group who may have been moved by *this* lesson to respond *this week* in a tangible way.

Sometimes a whole group will be moved by one particular lesson to do a major project in light of their deepened understanding of, and commitment to, God's will. Such a response would be well worth the weeks of study that may have preceded it.

Examples of life response activities:

1. A whole class, after studying Scriptural principles of evangelism, decides to host an outreach Bible study in a new neighborhood.

2. As a result of studying one of Paul's prayers for the Ephesians, a group member volunteers to start and oversee a church prayer chain for responding to those in need.

3. A group member invites others to join her in memorizing the key verse for the week.

4. Two group members, after studying portions of the Sermon on the Mount, write and perform a song about peacemaking.

Obviously, only you and your group can decide how to respond appropriately to the challenge of living for Christ daily. But the possibilities are endless.

[1]From *Using the Bible in Groups,* by Roberta Hestenes.
© Roberta Hestenes 1983. Adapted and used by permission of Westminster Press, Philadelphia, PA.

[2]The material on discussion methods is adapted from *Creative Teaching Methods,* by Marlene D. LeFever, available from your local Christian bookstore or from David C. Cook Publishing Co., 850 N. Grove Ave., Elgin, IL 60120. Order number: 25254. $14.95. This book contains step-by-step directions for dozens of methods appropriate for use in adult classes.